MW01268260

MEMORIES
— & —
MUSINGS

AN
ANTHOLOGY
BY
VINTAGE
MINNESOTANS

Compiled by Rachel R Johnson & Cathy Peterson on Behalf of Authors

Pieces written by The Whitney Writers and Poets

Design and distribution by Bublish

ISBN: 978-1-647046-86-6 (eBook)
ISBN: 978-1-64704-718-4 (paperback)

FOREWORD

By Steven M. Hoover, PhD

The volume you hold in your hands is a child of the pandemic. It was born of the need to connect at a time when social isolation and loneliness, especially among elders, was front and center in our collective awareness. In the early days of the pandemic, the Whitney Senior Center in Saint Cloud, Minnesota worked with me to begin offering a Guided Autobiography Class through Zoom to foster connections. The class has since been offered almost continuously, and it has been a great source of joy for me. I have been blessed with the unique opportunity to hear the wonderful stories shared by so many who have participated in the program. As restrictions were lifted, we moved to offering the class in-person, and among the early participants were Cathy and Rachel, Co-managers of this volume. After raising the idea of a collection of stories from the Guided Autobiography classes, they took the ball. They secured grant funding, solicited stories, and invited Jerry Wellik and his Poetry classes. The result of their efforts is *Memories and Musings: An Anthology by Vintage Minnesotans*. Like a fine, vintage wine, these stories should be savored—enjoyed slowly and contemplatively. You will find humor, sadness, and above all, connections. You may even be inspired to write your own stories or join one of our classes. Please do. We have a great time, and everyone is welcome. It really isn't about the writing; it's about the connections. Enjoy!

Only connect! That was the whole of her sermon. Only connect the prose and the passion, and both will be exalted, and human love will be seen at its height. Live in fragments no longer.

—E.M. Forster, *Howards End*

ACKNOWLEDGMENTS

Our sincere thanks to Steve Hoover and Jerry Wellik for their committed and continued leadership in the Guided Autobiography course and the ongoing Poetry group.

And our genuine thanks to the following for their funding and support:

- The Whitney Senior Center administration and staff for their continued efforts and help with this huge undertaking.
- The anonymous gift given to the GAB program through the Area Agency on Aging.
- The Central Minnesota Arts Board and staff for their support and belief in our project.
- The Whitney Writers and Poets and their families.

"This activity is made possible by the voters of Minnesota through a grant from the Central MN Arts Board, thanks to a legislative appropriation from the arts and cultural heritage fund."

CONTENTS

PART 3

Pathways of Family Memories

PART 4

Passages through Life's Journey

INTRODUCTION

This literary work has evolved from our involvement in the Whitney Senior Center's Guided Autobiography (GAB) course taught by Dr. Steve Hoover. As co-managers of this book project, we have been profoundly pleased with the participation and support of the Whitney Writers and Poets group that was created through this process. Without them, we wouldn't have been able to fill the pages of this anthology.

This project gives voice to the Central Minnesota vintage agers. We believe this one-of-a-kind achievement allows others to witness the lives, lessons, and transitions made by golden agers. Our vision was to publish a collection by seniors in Central Minnesota and to leave a cultural legacy for current and future generations.

That vision came to fruition with a grant award from the Central Minnesota Arts Board to help fund this venture. We are proud to share these treasured memories.

—Rachel Johnson and Cathy Peterson, Project Co-managers

PART

1

PATHS INTO CREATIVE WRITING

WORDS

By Rachel Johnson

My passion is for words.

In a book, on a napkin, falling like jewels from mouths.

Words curling across a page in script, words typed in quiet efficiency, or hiding behind an idea in my mind.

Words can be descriptors or say nothing while presuming to say something.

Words turn a pretty phrase or conjure ugly visions.

Words in my world make the world go round, yet have the capacity to still it on its axis.

Words are written, spoken, shouted, or they lurk below the surface as an unspoken message.

Words have formed me since I was a child—the good, the bad, and the ones I wish I hadn't said or heard.

Words communicate. Words teach. Words hurt. Words open worlds and wounds. Then close them.

Words can cascade from the mouth like a rushing river or dribble off the tongue in an awkward apology.

Words can be spoken in loud exhortations, slide across the lips in silky lies, or flit across a thought as a

shining, glimmering truth just realized.

Words have accompanied me through thick and thin, guided me, and deserted me, then bubbled up to

to the surface of my imagination, been captured, and been let go.

Words. Are. My. Passion.

THE POWER OF POETRY

By Jannine Provinzino

A poem is a concise verse of lines or stanzas, rhyming or not,
Proclaiming a message for the reader.
Why do we cherish a poem?
Poetry, in its rhythmic form, may soothe us,
Or it may stir up our emotions.
Poetry may relate a critical story or feeling.
It may guide us to grieve, to heal, to meditate, to find joy,
To see the beauty of nature, or it may even call us to action.
A poem may reflect truth, despair, sorrow, serenity, grace, love,
And so much more beyond our understanding.
The power of poetry, in all its forms, may simply be beyond measure.

BOOKS, BOOKS,
THE LOVE OF READING

By Cathy Peterson

When young, I was fortunate my parents believed in education. By the time I was seven years old, they had purchased a set of Childcraft books along with the World Book Encyclopedias. My sister and I knew they'd been expensive, and we cherished them. The Childcraft books arrived as a set of fifteen volumes containing everything imaginable a child could want: delightful nursery rhymes, poems, fairy tales, and other stories we all remember. The volumes were filled with wonderful illustrations, too. We never tired of them, nor did our neighbors. It wasn't long before the pages were worn and tattered.

One of our neighbors, Paul, the son of our band director, who lived kitty-corner behind us, entered our home daily in search of the encyclopedias. He was a brilliant child who never seemed to get enough information into his inquisitive brain. As a four-year-old, he could read everything and was a child of never-ending questions. He'd study the books for hours each day. He never wanted to play outside and instead preferred sitting in front of our bookcase! Of course, we thought he was weird at the time, but when I think back, maybe he was way ahead of the rest of us.

While in elementary school, our neighborhood group would take a weekly stroll to our town's library, which was only two blocks away. The library was an old, bulky, two-story, brick home with a sizeable porch out front. It was scary entering the building, as the nervous librarian was older than the house, and she only wore long, dark-colored dresses and black heels that clunked across the wooden floors. She always followed us to make sure we were behaving. Our older neighbor friends protected us and showed us all the possibilities in that bleak place.

The beautiful woodwork inside the library was a deep, dark-chestnut color. It framed the entire first floor and the many, many shelves that reached the ceiling. After going there a few times, and feeling a bit more relaxed, I found the Nancy Drew series written by Carolyn Keene. I fell in love with these mystery novels, and it wasn't long before I had read all of them.

By the time I was in high school and writing papers for English class, I realized the wealth of information we had right in our living room. This was a time before the internet, before computers even, but we had our encyclopedias! I could research most anything. I became grateful for my parents' sacrifice for our future endeavors in education. I know having those special books played a part in my receiving good grades in school. While the encyclopedias are long gone, their existence in our home will forever be remembered.

An author I became enamored with when I was fourteen was Margaret Mitchell. Her book *Gone with the Wind* brought me into the pre–Civil War era of the opulent South and then into the midst of the Civil War in the 1860s. More than fifty years later, the book can still occupy my thoughts. Its vivid setting of the magnificent plantations with their front porch columns, the tall and sturdy oak trees, the weeping willows dripping with moss, the grandeur of the winding staircases, the lavish gowns, the prosperous estate owners, and the deprived slaves living in meager conditions did something to my soul. I had the privilege of seeing the movie in the Cinemax theater in Minneapolis when I was fifteen. The huge, rounded screen was phenomenal, but the movie just couldn't compare to my imagination of the individuals living through the events in that book. It will always remain a favorite of mine.

Then, through much of my adult life, I didn't read much. I was caught up with being a good mom. I read a few books about parenting, especially those by Dr. Spock, and I read to my growing daughters, but it seems I was too busy to read books for myself. Spending time with my daughters was precious.

The book that really brought me back to reading was *The Da Vinci Code* by Dan Brown. His imagination (or truth?) of the bloodline of Christ and the mysteries of the church hiding facts to control people was a true inspiration, and the story enthralled me. I've read all of his books and have watched *The Da Vinci Code* movie many times. While Tom Hanks doesn't fit my imagination of the main character, the adaptation is still excellent in a myriad of ways.

Over the past ten years, my zest for books has grown immensely. While I still love mysteries, I have a love of paranormal and spirituality books. One such author I greatly appreciate is Neale Donald Walsch. His *Conversations with God* series are the most inspiring books I have ever read. His books, which contain a new look at spirituality and defining God, are so impactful and thought-provoking. I have also devoured the books written by Edgar Cayce. He was gifted with healing talents, without having any medical education.

There are so many authors I have valued and respected these past years, such as the mystery writer Catherine Coulter. Her novels keep you riveted and immersed in the story, to the point that you can't put them down, as the suspense mesmerizes you. I also want to continue to read the romantic works of JoAnn Ross, Nora Roberts, and Danielle Steele, which wouldn't be complete without bringing in human lust. I just finished a lengthy book in which two unfortunate, eccentric people found love amid their life trials, and their happy ending made me smile and shed a few tears. These stories bring personal memories to light to ponder anew. Then these new books, these friends we've gotten to know, live in our hearts forever.

I shall never stop reading, and I prefer to own my books so I can treasure them in my home. Most of the I own are used, but that fits my personality of saving a dime being thrifty. The covers may have become ragged, but the words inside remain the same and will continue to for years to come.

I read more and more through the pandemic, and this quote by Mason Cooley, a professor emeritus at the College of Staten Island, pretty much says it all: "Reading gives us some place to go when we have to stay where we are." So always keep a book close at hand.

BOOKS,BOOKS!

Books, books, such magical things.

How could I ever live without them when each one a new thought brings?

They surround me with vivid women and charming men,

Pleasant thoughts from days gone by, or crises and the emotional trauma of human life.

My thoughts wander and I ask how, what, where, why?

I have ventured through many trials and strife.

Books are the answer, so keep many of them near. Delve into one now and have no fear!

THE END!

THE NEW POETS

By J Vincent Hansen

We are the new poets.

We choose our causes carefully:
out of jail by nine,
back to the coffeehouse by ten.

We are the new poets.

We love from a distance/
We arrive at the finish
sans callous and scar.

We are the new poets.

We think our seat belts can save us
when the comfort of the seat
left us dead long ago.

STORY REFLECTIONS

By Rachel Johnson

We are a product of our surroundings and our past, and those things influence our future. Families, since the beginning of time, have found a way to relate those important lessons to those closest to them. It is the story of time. It is the story of a people. It is a story that is written in our DNA and our RNA, the staircases that built humanity. It is the story of us.

I listen to music on the stereo. It is the story of the composer and the musicians, shared with the listeners. For a moment in time, we all share the same experience, and that music and those composers and musicians become a part of our story. Music is a collection of reflections and stories that bind.

I was embroidering a flour sack towel. I had ironed on a black-lined transfer and was now filling in those lines. My friend joined me with her own embroidery. We had decided this year's project would be stitching pictures on towels as Christmas gifts. We sat across from each other, filling in those black lines with color and stitches. Sometimes we sat in silence. Sometimes we chatted. Little by little, those strands of colored floss were lovingly woven into a picture telling the story of the stitcher and the giftee. The day was a story in itself—of friendship and embroidery, white towels and colored floss. A plain towel, finally bursting to life with a story. Two friends quietly sharing of themselves. A story of two.

I sit with my thoughts. Yesteryear's stories and plans for the present are swirling together. A textile of sadness, happiness, and expectation merging and separating. Stories and more stories, some shared, some too painful to share. Life, life, and more life hiding behind my eyes. But a smile can dispel anything. Smiles and stories shared and not shared. Smiles and stories like a tornado of time. Smiles and smiles and more smiles. Stories written and stories not written, spinning and dancing about my mind like a whirligig.

Stories become history, and history becomes ancient. People are born, and people live their lives, and people's lives pass by and become ancestors of their own story. Children pass down what they have learned from their families—the good, the bad, and the ugly. My Grandma Clark taught me to sew and embroider, but, because of her experience, would not teach me tatting. My Grandma Nora taught me superstitions, how to have and share fun, how to be a good grandma. We all have these stories of our loved ones. We all pass them down. They become oral stories. Stories are the stuff of love and life. Stories are histories. Stories are in our DNA and our RNA.

Look at a stranger. Look in their eyes. You can see their story written across their being. Joy or pain, happiness or sadness. Sometimes you can look in someone's eyes and see nothing—nothingness to their soul. We all have a story to tell. A story to remember or a story we cannot forget. It is a part of the human condition. Stories on canvas, stories on a flour sack towel, stories of friendship, stories of war, stories that tell themselves.

We are walking books, chapter and verse emanating from deep within. All we have to do is look or feel. We are the story of us. Each story one of a kind. Classes like this guided autobiography one make us look ourselves in the face and try to enunciate our own story. Even if we cannot do so outright, we can do so internally. If we are losing our memories, these classes can pull the stories from the abyss of a fading mind, giving comfort in the sharing of themselves before the veil descends.

Stories and storied. Memory and memories. Colors and emotions. Humanity and human frailties. You can hear them when no one is talking. You can feel them when no one is touching you. They are there. Whispering from the past. Shouting into the present. Echoing from tomorrow. They are the stories of us. Stories of them. Stories of those who are not yet here. All you have to do is listen with your heart and soul.

Reflections from Main Street

By J Vincent Hansen

This brash young man
Sinclair Lewis,
whose claim to fame
was that he knew us ~

like little pieces
of dirty wash,
hung us out
for posterity to bash.

Then citing
intellectual atrophy,
moved off
to live in Italy,

where he died
alone, morose, and weary ~
perhaps he should have
stayed in Gopher Prairie.

HAIKU

By Rachel Johnson

profile of darkness
under arcs of light, shadow
following me, mine

CRACKS

By Faye Schreder

There are words we speak and words we see.
What could the meaning of these words be?

There's the crack of dawn and a crack in the wall,
The crack of a bat that connects with a ball.

You can crack a nut or crack a joke,
Crack the whip or crack the case.

The ice will crack on a frozen lake.
The crack of a gun will start the race.

There are wisecracks and plumbers' cracks,
Cracks of thunder and Cracker Jacks.

There are tough nuts to crack and crackpots, too.
A crack in your voice when you're feeling blue.

If you're a cop after crooks, you'll be cracking down.
You'll crack folks up if you're a clown.

Words, words, words, more than we've ever heard.
What are the meanings of all these silly words?

2

TRAILS AND TRACKS IN NATURE

THE LOON

By Ann Romanowsky

You were still in the nest on Mother's Day,
Newly hatched on Father's Day.
You rode, safe and snug, on your parents' back
Not yet ready for water so cold and deep.

By the Fourth of July you were swimming,
Paddling your black, webbed feet.
Down, down you went
catching minnows in your beak.

There is much to learn before you fly.
Where to fish and how to survive.
The plaintive tremolo answers softly
Time now to spread your wings.

Photo by Ann Romanowsky

ANIMAL SPACE

By Elena Bookstrom White

How strange my disconnection!
I feel as curious about the stories
my friends tell about their dear animal friends
as about those strangely distant forest animals.

The barky waggy slobbery nippy dogs,
the furry purry lap kitties
with their unpredictable claws,
I prefer to hold distant.

Ah! It's *my* animal impulse
to shy away
from such close intrusion
or to stand
at a safe distance, inquiring
like a deer.

Wait! Was that a fox?
A hint of triangle face?
Fleeting, fleeing magic!

THE EARTH MOVED!

By Jean Eulberg-Steffenson

Really, what was all the commotion? I woke from a deep sleep like someone shook me awake. It was very dark, and I heard my husband rummaging around in our room in Puerto Rico. I saw his phone light up as he typed a message to our son, Matt, in Australia. "We had an earthquake at 4:45 a.m. The power is out!" My brain started to interpret this message as I struggled through my grogginess. What? My husband shined a flashlight, then informed me there had been a major earthquake just south of us and the power was out throughout Puerto Rico. We had many messages urging us to go home and a message from my friend in the Virgin Islands urging us to leave and visit them immediately.

My husband, Greg, and I discussed the situation. Though the power was off across all of Puerto Rico, the damage was a long way south of us. We didn't know how long the power would be off. We had reservations at a high-rise in Luquillo for the next three nights, which was forty-five miles away. My husband reached the owner, who said the power should be back on by then. Since no stoplights were working, my husband decided against driving the car we had rented. Luckily, we were able to reach an uber driver, who drove us to the apartment complex. After we were dropped off, we found out there was *not* an elevator that worked for our fourteenth-floor rental! My husband called the owner, who allowed us to find another place and not get charged. We were fortunate to find a small, two-story hotel across from the ocean that had a generator and had breakfast included with the stay! We even found a restaurant for lunch down the street. However, that evening, they were out of food, and everything else was closed, including grocery stores. I begged our hotel staff for something to eat, and they gave us some bread and peanut butter. It was delicious!

We had signed up for a snorkeling trip the next day. We joined a group, and between stops, we talked with a young couple. They were staying in the high-rise where we were supposed to stay! Since they had no power, they had to walk up and down sixteen floors with buckets of water to flush the toilet! I really couldn't imagine it! Just the thought of it exhausted me!

Then it was off to Ceiba, where we had a unique, retired Brooklyn cop for a driver. She was a large lady with long, thick, black hair who looked stuffed into her small, shiny blue car. She had a never-ending story combined with her own laugh track. Before driving us, she'd had to unload her car, which had been packed up for a tsunami (which never came). Unfortunately, her blended Brooklyn and New York accent was affected by a large tongue stud that compromised our ability to understand her. She described herself as a tour guide. However, she mainly shared stories of a boyfriend intent on harming her, a father who was attempting to hurt his new wife, and cousins who were thieves, along with frightening stories of the area as we "toured." She rarely pointed out any landmarks! Though we did manage to observe some beautiful views. We put in a long day of listening to her perspectives of life while we ate at her favorite spots and listened to her tales. One involved her peeing on the floor of the restaurant we were at. I think I lost my appetite! After each stop, Greg and I fought for the back seat so we could tune out. I argued that he needed the front seat for leg room, but he quickly crawled in the back anyway! After our "tour" day, we planned to head to the ferry the next morning, with the same driver. At 3:00 a.m., I received a message that she was in the hospital due to asthma. We asked the landlord of the place where we were staying for a recommendation and finally found a different driver. Oh my!

We took a ferry and relaxed for a few days in lovely Vieques. We did *not* have a "tour guide." We rented a golf cart and headed for the beach and some other areas. We dined on delicious food. We stayed in a hostel (my husband found it). The room was very plain, and the communal kitchen had seen better days. But there was an attached restaurant, which was great, and we were located by the ocean. So, we could relax in scenic surroundings.

Then we had to return to Ceiba and our "tour guide." We were grateful to see her and listen to her stories as she drove us to San Juan for our flight and were glad she'd made it out of the hospital. Puerto Rico had returned somewhat to normal, with traffic lights working and such. We attempted to block out the stories.

Before flying out, we stayed one night in San Juan with an extremely kind gentleman, who was retired and rented mainly for the company. We could wash all of our clothes, use his kayak, and eat where he recommended. He also helped us get to the airport the next day. He was a treasure!

Then, we flew to Saint Croix to stay with one of my friends from high school, Janet, and her husband, Lon. We relaxed, laughed a lot, and enjoyed the amazing sights and culture of Saint Croix. The days were extremely hot, but after a long hike, we could jump in the ocean. Ahhh! We listened as the talented Lon put on a great concert for everyone who lived in their condo complex. We had a few minor disappointments as well. After driving through a powerful rainstorm to get to a concert, we found out it was canceled. After hearing rave reviews on some restaurants, we arrived at them to find them closed! I think Greg and I brought bad luck with us! Ha! When we flew back and arrived in Minnesota, I felt relaxed after the stress we had felt from the earthquake. What a fool I was! It was January 2020.

Five weeks later, we flew to Australia. However, the trip ended quickly due to the pandemic. We left ten days early, relieved to have found a flight due to the airlines shutting down! With heavy hearts, we left our son, his wife, and our three grandchildren. We finally saw them two and a half years later. I had pondered if we should just stay there. Luckily we didn't, because two months later, I was diagnosed with a rare, aggressive breast cancer called triple-negative breast cancer. I'd had my annual mammogram three months later than usual. The radiologist informed me that if I'd had a mammogram on time, my cancer may not have appeared and wouldn't have been detected until next year's mammogram. "A year would have been too late," she said.

So, 2020 was not a relaxing, boring year for us. It was challenging, frightening, and filled with medical appointments. There was a very bright light for us, though. Our grandson Cal was born on February 27, in Minnesota, to our son, Chris, and his wife, Allison! A new life brought tremendous joy during this bleak time.

First Love

By Jerry Wellik

How could a horse be so single-minded?
Kellie's face etched inside his head
never goes away
sees her in rainbows and shadows
hears her voice in rain and wind
when he sees her, he snorts
that's his name for Kellie.

He snorts her name again
only name he knows
name of the apples and soap
oats and cold water
caressing his mane
feel of her hands on mouth
gripping legs on ribs.

Kellie mounts the forlorn beast
his sides become heaving bellows
nose a blowing locomotive
legs mighty wheels drawn straight
tail spouting steam
eyes shining spotlights
mane a snowstorm in her face.

Riding, they come together like clasped hands
pounding flesh and flashing blood
striking bones and beating brains
crossing and weaving together
licking the earth like a flame
pigs and chickens struck dumbfounded
beetles and moles convinced they've seen God.

BEAVER DREAMS (PART ONE)

By Jim Romanowsky

Home pond iced over
His beaver family
Huddled in the lodge
Long nights dozing
As wind and coyotes
Howl a call and response
Days spent on errands
Under the ice
Lodge maintenance
Raising the kits
Dreams of glory days
With the dam building crew
Before retiring
To this quiet backwater

Photo by Jim Romanowsky

BEAVER DREAMS (PART TWO)

By Jim Romanowsky

I read that if you can get near a beaver lodge in the winter, if the light is right, you can see the vapor from their breaths coming up through the ventilation hole, and you may even be able to hear the sounds they make to interact with each other. Gotta try that this winter!

Overheard at the Beaver Lodge ventilation hole:

The wife says, "I gotta go for a swim. The kits are driving me crazy!"
Yeah, kits these days! Can't tell 'em a dam thing!
Bunch of little gnaw-it-alls.
Got no respect for the alders.
Oh well . . .
Pass me another willow branch
Wood ja?

Photo by Jim Romanowsky

Beaver Dreams (Part Three)

By Jim Romanowsky

Dreaming of a tree like this
To sink your teeth into next spring?
Pick up an issue of *Chopper's Weekly*
Or log onto our webbed site @flattailtales
For locations and availability.
We also feature cutting-edge fashions
And incisive reporting on issues
Near and dear to the
Wood eater's heart.

—Jim (who appreciates your furbearance of the Beaver Dreams triad)

Beaver Dreams (Part Four)

By Jim Romanowsky

The lodge seems still in winter
But tracks don't lie.
For midnight patrols
It's the place to be.
Where emissaries
Emit scent messages
To be downloaded
By sentries
To olfactory files
Plotting a New Pond Order
Come spring?
If so, they're
Keeping it quiet.

Photo by Jim Romanowsky

AN ODE TO WHISPERING WOODS*

By Roseanna Gaye Ross

Ancient hills
Rolling rows of birch, oak, pine, elm, maple
Rippling up hills and into valleys—
Intertwined threads of gold and crimson glisten in the autumn sun.

Here, native elders narrated stories of bountiful harvests, triumphant hunts.
Here, native mothers suckled babies and buried their dead in craggy
    sandstone caves.

Here, pioneer families hewed logs for shelter, and mothers rocked babies
    to the flickering light of kerosene lamps.
Here, horse rustlers concealing their stolen prize, positioned atop the open-
    mouthed caves, watched for their captors.

Now, coyotes howl a lullaby from the hollows to the sparkling stars.
From behind a thin vale of tall brown grass, a buck snorts a greeting to
    the dawn.
The hawk swoops and cries out to the skies in the heat of the afternoon sun.

The woods whisper secrets still not heard.

Their soft breath gently tickles to life the dancing leaves of the white-
    barked birch
Exposing their silver underbellies to the sun.
The sweet sound of their rustling murmurs teases the air.

I am called to this sacred space
    Like a sailor to a siren's song
    Like a child to her mother's arms.

Here, my ears see, my eyes listen.

The woods whisper secrets I long to know.

*Whispering Woods refers to my Ohio farmland.

SNAKES

By Steven M. Hoover, PhD

When I was seven or eight, I was staying at my grandparents' cottage (in Indiana, they were not called cabins) for a week. While playing in the woods near their cottage, I found a nest of five small baby snakes. I put them in a shallow box and brought them into the front room of the cottage, which had a stone fireplace, to play with. My grandfather noticed and simply said to be sure I took them back outside before Grandma got home from the store, as she hated snakes. Typical for a child, I quickly lost interest and wandered off, leaving the snakes in the front room. When my grandpa noticed the empty box, he asked me if I had taken the snakes outside, and I indicated that I had. My lie was exposed when my grandmother returned, screamed, and started swearing (I learned some new words that day). Quickly, I rushed around to collect the three snakes she had spotted and put them outside. Yes, three of five. I never told them there were still two somewhere in the cottage. I spent the week quietly searching for, but never finding, the missing two. Years later, my mother was sitting in the front room when a snake crawled out of the stone fireplace and into the room. It was an adult snake . . .

Opening the Lake House

By Deb McAlister

On a bleak April day,
I drive to the lake house
To meet the plumber.
The snow is gone,
But the trees and fields are still barren.
My key turns the lock.
It is cold and dark inside.
I open the shades to reveal
The frozen lake and colorless landscape.

But beneath the crust of ice, as the ice fishers know, the lake is not barren.
And only a few days ago, I stood with my church community and sang,
With choir and organ and brass, celebrating the miracle of resurrection.
My faith tells me that soon this gloomy landscape
Will be transfigured with color,
And warm summer days will come
When I will be immersed in the cool water,
Splashing and playing with my children and grandchildren,
A baptism of joy and hope.

A STEER IN SCHOOL

By Faye Schreder

Our family lived close to our country school, so we had to run home at noon to eat. We didn't consider it a boon, because when we got back, sides were usually drawn for the ball game behind the schoolhouse and other games were already underway.

One day, my cousin Ray walked home at noon, too. He pulled some fat carrots from his mother's garden and gnawed on them while he put a halter on his pet steer, then led it down the gravel road to school. I was coming back from my house and met him in the schoolyard.

"Why are you bringing Hayseed to school?" I asked.

"He wanted to come to school!" Ray grinned, scratching the animal between its horns. "Do you think we could get him into the schoolhouse?"

"Sure. I'll help," I volunteered.

Ray pulled two ears of corn from the pockets of his bib overalls, and we nine-year-olds went to work. I set the corn on the first five steps and waited breathlessly while Ray quietly led Hayseed to the golden bait. As they approached, I moved it a step higher. The steer snorted nervously but followed the corn. Another step, I moved it again. His hooves scraped and slid awkwardly as he strove to maintain a footing on the concrete steps, determined to reach the delectable treat.

Soon, swings emptied, jump ropes sprawled in the grass, and baseball gloves dropped as groups of students became absorbed in the drama.

"Shhh," Ray cautioned, "Don't spook 'im or he'll run."

Speaking softly, Ray patiently coaxed Hayseed until the steer, tail twitching nervously, reached the final step. "Careful now—open the door and move the corn into the cloakroom," Ray instructed in barely a whisper.

We were about to cross the threshold into the entryway when *ding-ding-ling*! Our teacher stepped out ringing the handheld brass school bell. It was hard to tell who was more startled, the children, the city-bred teacher, or the five-hundred-pound Hereford that bolted down the steps and across the schoolyard, plopping giant, green "pies" on the steps as calling cards!

Ray took off in pursuit of his steer. When he finally caught him, he tied him to a tree. Then, as an afterthought, he ran back for the corn and dropped it on the ground in front of his pet.

Meanwhile, our teacher carefully steered her charges up the messy steps and settled them down to begin afternoon classes.

When Ray walked in, she snapped at him, "Use the shovel from the coal room to clean up the mess . . . and wash it at the pump when you're finished."

Ray got back from his chore just in time for arithmetic class.

Stifling a giggle, he whispered to me, "Hayseed wouldn't have made a mess if he hadn't been frightened by the sound of that darn bell!"

At afternoon recess, the teacher said, "You're all excused to go out to play—except Faye and Ray. You two will stay inside and do arithmetic problems on page thirty-eight."

The crack of bat against ball and singsong chants of girls skipping rope floated through the open windows while our teacher lectured us.

"And Faye," she added with indignation, "You're a girl, and girls just don't do this sort of thing!"

We two renegades sneaked a glance at each other's freckled faces as if to say, "The fun was well worth the trouble!"

CASTING FOR

By Mardi Knudson

lake map loaded in GPS
red portable gas tank full
AlumaCraft "Queen of the Waterways"
ready to slide off once white trailer
9.8 horse vintage black Merc clamped on transom
leech bag writhing
twenty-pound Power Pro line wound on
Shamano spinning reel
forecast encourages
Bud Light Lime wrapped in cozi
salami/mustard sandwich packed in cooler
boat launches down cement ramp
quest begins
rod grip melds to palm
casts easily
hours
idle
by
breeze carries sun's warmth
shoulders sag
eyelids droop behind polarized sun glasses
concerns gently rock away with lake ripples
stringer empty
I got what I came for

OUR WILD VISITORS

By Ann Romanowsky

Our wild visitors
brought the thrill of nature
to our quiet neighborhood.

Their only job strutting, scratching,
rising up to show off their feathers
in a Spring display.

They are not required
to search their hearts
for a higher purpose.

Just being themselves, beaks down,
digging for bugs,
they find what they are looking for.

Photo by Ann Romanowsky

I AWAKE

By Mardi Knudson

The morning we enter the BWCA with anticipation,
Zipways clean, legs bite free. Senses
heighten while loading packs and
canoes. Routine route for leeches.
Breakfast and permit. As we
near our lake entry point,
paddlers reflect silently on
this adventure's possibilities.
Plan's reviewed, maps folded.
Canoes and water embrace on
entry. We dance effortlessly
across a ripple-free lake. Dragonflies
guide over portages. Rhythmic paddling
unburdens soul. Images store like a photo album in
my memory: a bloated, fly-covered moose, purple-blue
sunsets silhouetting majestic pines, contented feeling
of solitude as we sit by our evening campfire on a lichen-
covered granite rock. In this pristine wilderness, my eyes
are opened, and *I awaken to a new enlightenment.*

POTATOLOGY

A TREATISE ON ESTRANGEMENT
By J Vincent Hansen

One man will till his plot and plant his potatoes in spring,
will and hoe through the long hot summer
and wrestle to his cellar in autumn
the bulging burlap bags ~

Another man will buy his potatoes at a supermarket ~

Another man eats french fries at a fast-food restaurant ~

Another man eats potato chips purchased for him
by the government ~

And so it is that a child becomes a fetus
and the fetus becomes tissue
and the tissue, nuisance.

AUTUMN LOVE

By Cathy Peterson

Spin me like the rushing wind
Under the rust-colored autumn leaves
As the trees reach up their branched arms
Upward to the cloud-covered heavens
Lazily releasing their growth of the season.

Take my hand and dance with me
Under the brilliance of the harvest colors
As they seep into my spirited soul
Twirling in a musical spiral essence
Creating a deep red fiery emotion.

Wrap me in your arms with your warm embrace
Feeling God's aura and invisible breath
While the sun sends its illuminating rays.
Its sumptuous splendor cheers the way
Bringing forth a passion of the crisp day.

Take my desire and lay me down
Unto the nestled softness of the dried earth.
Fill me with your bountiful rhapsody
As our pounding hearts beat together
Like the rhythm of the long-ago native drums.

Sensing the fragrance of the autumn air
Touching the crimson and golden hues
Surrounding our earthbound joys
Joined in pleasures that reap such sensual powers.
My season, my hope, harvest's wonder of destiny.

YOUTH

By Ann Romanowsky

They grow up so fast; a recurring refrain
referencing our continued surprise.
Life seldom proceeds at our expected pace.

Bodies and feathers grow, horizons expand,
And young ones set forth,

Into a world unhampered by our limitations.
A flight path never before navigated.

Sun and moon for sextant,
They arrive in a new land.

Photo by Ann Romanowsky

Squirrel Dances

By Elena Bookstrom White

*The Scamper**

In nature's fun scene from my window,
the squirrels go round, they go round up and down,
the scratch and the scrabble of toenails on trees
stretching their bellies (two chasing, one stopping),
its tail flick-a-flicking, chittering and
chattering while the first races on, swinging
and falling and flipping, still running, her
shanks are so quick to catch onto
the branches, such chances, what dances!
in nature's fun scene from my window.

*Inspired by "The Dance," a poem by William Carlos Williams in response to Pieter Brueghel's painting, *Kermesse* (1567-68)

Caesura
I see two squirrels
Each one resting on a branch
Afternoon slow down

Solo
A snow laden branch
Stripped by a running squirrel
Snow spray in sunlight

AUTUMN

By Jannine Provinzino

Colors expanding in bright bursts of red, orange, gold, and yellow,
Such abundant splendor sharing a glorious landscape in wondrous harmony with glory and awe.

If only people in all our diverse and varied shades and colors:
Black, brown, red, and tan, could also share and embrace such beauty with peace and love.

FULL CIRCLE OUT OF THE DIRT

By Cathy Peterson

Dad's best friend was called Doc for short. He was a small, strongly built, energetic man who was always inventing something, thus the name "Doctor of Inventions" fit him well. He loved Native American artifacts and hunting for them, and he loved archery, too.

His main invention in the 1960s, which he was able to patent and brought his business into a profit-making enterprise, was an item called a Snaro. It's a hunting device in the form of an arrow end designed with a large surface area, instead of a point, that resembles a cloverleaf of wire. It screws into the end of the arrow, and its purpose is to increase one's odds of hunting success by tangling up a bird's wings to bring them to the ground. A flat-nose, centered, blunt end delivers a killing shock instead of tearing a bird (or fish) apart, so that it can still be used for eating. The Snaro was a great success, and they can still be purchased today.

In addition, Doc had an arrow-making business, so the Snaros could be purchased with or without the hand-painted wooden or fiberglass arrows. His archery building, complete with an archery range, had plenty of space where employees could work on the arrows. While in junior high, my sister and I were hired to help paint arrows. Anyone ordering arrows could decide on the color and length. It was quite fun holding the thin paint brush as the arrows revolved on a spinning machine made from old treadle sewing machines (another invention) we had to push with our feet. We each also got to paint our own designs, as we were actively involved in learning archery, too, and had our own bows along with the uniquely colored arrows.

But I need to back up a bit here. As I mentioned, Doc was an avid treasure and artifact collector. My sisters and I would occasionally be invited to tag along with my dad and Doc on their hunting excursions, out to the dirt of the harvested fields in the country.

One dreary, cold Saturday morning in late October when I was twelve, my sisters and I were told we could accompany Dad and Doc out to a farm field near the small village of Avoca, seven miles away. Despite the cold, I jumped at the chance to go, as did my younger sister, but my older sister declined. The field we arrived at was located on an old lake bed where the Dakota Sioux tribes supposedly would have set up an encampment more than several hundred years ago. I was so excited to search for the revered arrowheads we were always stalking the fields for.

In the fall, after harvest, was the perfect time to search for the arrowheads, as the dirt was newly plowed and turned over. It was a bit difficult walking through the muddy clumps, but I was ready with my boots on. After an hour and a half, I was tired and cold and had found no arrowheads. Then, as I trudged along, I spotted something red and hard inside a crusted mass of dirt. I showed it to Doc, who responded, "Oh, it's nothing. Just toss it away." Well, this was the only thing I'd found, so instead of tossing it, I tucked it into my coat pocket. I was too curious to see what might be under all the dirt. The red stone looked like it might be a bit of pipestone.

It was pipestone, and this newly found object was a little hand-carved pipe! This special object ended up being the find of the day! It measured about three and a half inches long. It was an ancient item that I now treasured. I truly believed I was the one meant to find it. The small pipe fit so perfectly in my hand. Question after question about it entered my mind. Was I the one who had carved it, perhaps as a young teen in another life? When was it made? What had the lake and encampment looked like back then? I imagined being there on a crisp, cool day, lying in a tepee with smoke billowing out the top.

Then, when I was nineteen, after my parents' divorce, my mother sold our home and moved away. The pipe went missing. I was quite devastated and even accused my mom of giving it to Doc. She said she hadn't. Doc said he didn't have it. It became an ongoing mystery my mind never lost sight of.

Many years later, upon taking my second daughter to visit my younger sister in San Francisco as a gift for receiving her master's degree, the mystery came to an end. My sister confessed she had been jealous of me finding the pipe, and when she and my mom had moved, she had stolen it. She felt the anguish of guilt and was filled with remorse for doing so. Her apology was easily accepted, as I was so thrilled just to have it back. The pipe had now been returned to me after having lots of miles and years put on it! It had come full circle out of the dirt, traveled cross-country to Las Vegas, then on to San Francisco, and back into my hands to fly home to Southwest Minnesota, where the red stone from its creation exists.

Upon returning home, my first goal was to go out and find a special leather pouch for the cherished pipe. It would never again leave me (hopefully). We had now been through a reunion, and joy was the outcome. This object was now a part of my spiritual journey. This item I found at a young age has heightened and broadened my love of antiques and ancient artifacts to this day. Through my life's quest, the pipe has also added to my beliefs in the spiritual world and to a better understanding of the daily lives of ancient Native tribes, which have always, I believe, revolved around the love, respect, and flow of nature and Mother Earth. It seems strange to allow part of my spirituality to be based on this hand-created object, but I have so much respect, reverence, and high regard for the Native tribes and their insight that all creatures are connected.

A few years ago, I sent photos of the little pipe to the archaeology department at the University of South Dakota, and I was told the pipe was possibly eight hundred to nine hundred years old. I also dedicate my interest in hunting artifacts to Doc, who passed just a month after my mom in 2020. I had kept in touch with him since my childhood.

It wouldn't be unusual to find me hunting around in the dirt with my metal detector on any given day, watching the television shows *Ancient Aliens* or *The Curse of Oak Island*, or reading about hidden treasures. My thoughts continue to delve into the many ancient mysteries worldwide that live under the dirt.

The Sequel

By Jim Romanowsky

To us, it just looks like
A spear fisherman's dark house.
But remember how
In STABBIN' CABIN #1
The hapless northern pike
Wanders under one
And it suddenly becomes
The BAITS MOTEL?

Photo by Jim Romanowsky

NIGHT SKI

By Ann Romanowsky

The woods are snowy, dark, and deep
The soft lights on the trail allow me to keep,
My skis in the grooves on the path ahead
To see my way without fear or dread.

I know the way; I've been here before,
Have skied this path in days of yore.
Mild winter temperatures and sunny days
Leave the soft kiss of winter on my face.

With thanks to Robert Frost's "Stopping by the Woods on a Snowy Evening"

Photo by Ann Romanowsky

A WINTER STORM

By James Ellickson

I believe we all have "branch points" in our history. If things had gone "the other way," we might never have existed. This first story is about one of my branch points.

In the winter of 1873, a January snowstorm was approaching Winnebago County in North Central Iowa. A father had walked to the nearest town, about six miles distance, for some reason no one can remember. As he was returning to his home, a neighbor stopped him and advised him that a storm was approaching and that he should stay with them, at least until it had passed by.

In the meantime, a mother at home and her three little children had used up their firewood and were looking around for a way to keep from freezing to death in the bitter cold and windy weather.

A grandfather, living a half mile away, stopped to check on the family. "Is anybody still living?" he called out as he approached the house.

He found a few fence posts and cut them up for firewood. Then they all huddled together. They survived the storm, and they were all reunited as a family after a three-day struggle with hunger and the winter weather. The children especially remembered how scared they all were during that terrible winter storm.

The oldest child was my grandmother, Katie Larson, who was about five years old at the time. Without her survival, I would not exist today. Everyone probably has a story like that, somewhere back in their history. My ancestors from Old Norway survived, so I can tell you this story today.

Greeting Seasons

By Elena Bookstrom White

Tiny glowing flames
Patch of red leaves in the woods
Lit by morning sun

Lone snowflake wanders
Down through the cold sunny air,
Lands on a lawn chair

Is it knit or purl?
The thick old vine loops over
And up toward the sun

Leaning and fallen
Old trees gather each snowstorm
Into peaceful puffs

Creek was snow covered
But today its ice gleams back
At the warming sun

Snowflakes flurrying
Speckling April's greening grass
Robins run and fly

A flittering flock
Chickadees chase like squirrels
Bright cardinal spectates

Heavy steam bath heat
Minnesota summertime
Breathing hot thickness

Morning ritual
My deadhead meditation:
Pinching spent blossoms

Lacy gold birch leaves
Remind me of home mountains
Gold coins on Aspens

RENEWAL

By Mardi Knudson

twigs, match, fire ignites
earthy smoke ascends to stars
reflecting back peace

Sunday Worship in God's Cathedral

By Ann Romanowsky

A Sunday morning walk in the cold white woods
Shows evidence of miracles afoot.
Life's most ancient cycle seen
In a tiny ribcage in a pile of scat.

One life ended in order to sustain
And nourish another
In a rhythm as old as time,
One species produces, another consumes.

A great horned owl in a bare oak tree,
A silent guardian of the forest,
It wings away from the branch
In a quiet whoosh.

Its nest nearby in another tree
Waiting in the pregnant pause
Before spring, the forest renew-
    ing itself
In the perpetual dance of
    creation.

Photo by Ann Romanowsky

PART

3

PATHWAYS OF
FAMILY MEMORIES

My Swedish Aunts

By Deb McAlister

I was a city girl, growing up in the suburbs of Minneapolis, where my parents both had teaching jobs. But I always felt a strong connection to my mother's family in rural Grant County, Minnesota. We visited them often while I was growing up. My beloved grandmother, my aunt and uncle and their children, and "the aunties" all lived there. The aunties were the four sisters of my Grandfather Nelson, who died when my mother was a young girl. She'd always been close to her aunts; they'd never married or had children of their own, and they doted on my mother, their favorite niece. The Nelson family had emigrated to Minnesota from Sweden in 1881, settling on a farm in the Wendell area. The five boys, including my grandfather, had left home as they came of age to make their way in the world, but the four daughters (Hannah, Anna, Magda, and Alma) had remained in the family home. Even after their parents died, the sisters stayed together. To my mother, and to me and my cousins of the next generation, they were always known as "the aunties."

The Nelson sisters grew to adulthood in the early part of the twentieth century. Why did the aunties never marry? For one thing, they were Swedes, a minority in a community dominated by Norwegian immigrants. It seems there was suspicion and distrust between the two groups, and mixed marriages were frowned upon. My mother heard them tell stories of gentlemen callers and even say that Magda had been engaged at one time, but for whatever reason, the sisters remained spinsters. Anna and Magda became teachers, and teachers in those days were forbidden to marry. They taught in small, rural schools in Minnesota and North Dakota, often staying with farm families when school was in session but always returning home by train during vacations and holidays. Hannah was a dressmaker, and she would go to people's homes to sew clothing for the family. Their mother had decided early on that the three older daughters were to find work outside the home but that Alma would remain at home and learn the art of Swedish cooking and baking and other homemaking skills.

Hannah died before I was born, but the other three aunts were in their sixties and living in a small house in Elbow Lake when my sister and I came into the picture. To me, the house was dark and smelled like "old people," but in the summer when the windows were open, it wasn't quite as bad. The living room had dark-wood furniture. Every end table had a crocheted doily on it, and there was a long high table by the window with Alma's collection of African violets in every shade of pink and purple. And there was a piano with a rotating stool. What fun for little girls who loved to plink and plunk on the keys and spin each other around! In the summer, my sister and I played in the large garden in the back, abounding with fragrant flowers and vegetables.

Alma was my favorite of the aunties. A small woman with wild, red, curly hair, a husky voice, and a sunny disposition, she was forever pinching our cheeks and calling us endearing names in Swedish. Her cheeks were always rosy (I still wonder if it was rouge or if that was her natural coloring). I remember the kitchen, Alma's domain, with its walk-in pantry, which always had tins of cookies and loaves of freshly baked bread. There were shelves with a colorful array of canned vegetables from the garden, jellies, jams, and fruit, which were very impressive to me since gardening and putting up food was not a part of our life in the city. I also recall a large crock that sometimes contained a thick, yogurt-like substance on top. Alma explained it came from milk that had soured while sitting in the crock for a few days. It sounded gross, but when she spooned it into delicate little bowls and sprinkled it with sugar and cinnamon, it was sublime!

Aunt Magda was much more serious, but she told interesting stories about her teaching career. And she had bookshelves with lots of books, including beautifully illustrated fairy tales in English and Swedish. I have gotten to know her better as an adult by reading her letters and yearbooks, which my mother saved. My sister and I, along with our mother, became teachers, influenced, I think, by Magda and her love of teaching. She was educated at St. Cloud Normal School, went back when it became St. Cloud Teacher's College, and eventually got a four-year teaching degree there.

I didn't know Anna well; she was older than the others and was always sick, in my memory. She didn't emerge from her bedroom often (the one room we were never allowed to enter). During one visit, I remember my mother and the aunts whispering about Anna's serious condition. It was disturbing to me to think of my aunt dying in that mysterious bedroom (which she did, shortly after that visit).

Of course, when I was young, my idea of a family was a father and a mother and children; this was reflected in my suburban neighborhood, families of my friends, and even my early readers at school (such as the Dick and Jane series). So, a family consisting of only women seemed quite unusual to me. But a family they were. They worked, supported themselves, and made a home and a life together. Alma even learned to drive and got a car when they moved to town—a rarity for a woman in those days—but it was a necessity, and she took it on. I know my mother, my sister, and I, and now my daughter, still benefit from the legacy of these strong, capable, loving women.

THE BOHEMIAN WAY

By Jerry Wellik

How do I choose
to Be in this world

The Bohemian Way
is the way for me

Exchanging stories
playing entertaining

laughing celebrating
every day a gift

beyond what's
previously imagined

fascinated with hobos
gypsies, outliers

ones longing
to be invited in

here's a kolache
coffee or tea

The Bohemian Way
is the way for me

Childhood Days on the Farm in Wisconsin 1945

By Patsy Magelssen

My older brother, Donnie, eight years my senior, went to school a mile and a half down the gravel road from our house. The school was a white, rectangular building with big windows on the sides. There was a porch on the front with a tower that held a large bell. This was rung when school was about to start to call the students in from play. There was a shelf with a basin and a pail of fresh water that had been pumped, where the students were to wash their hands as we came in. Pegs held their coats in a row, and there was a large box of wood for the fire.

Before school each day, the students formed a long line of kids going out to the wood pile and passed logs along to the teacher, who placed them in the wood box. You can imagine the laughter, pushing into the snow, and snowball fights that erupted while doing this. The back of the schoolroom held a very large, potbellied stove, which gave out warmth on the cold winter days. The teacher had to make the fire when she came in the morning. There was a large picture of George Washington on the left wall and a series of canvas, roll-down maps on the right wall.

There were clotheslines to hang up wet clothes and a place to set wet boots. Our wool snow pants, jackets, and hats got packed with snow during the long walk to school. They had to hang up to dry for the long walk home.

In the schoolyard, there was a merry-go-round with rods to hang on to. It had an indentation in the soil from kids going around and around, which filled up when it rained. "Chubby Allen" (he was proud of his nick-name) would get his tongue stuck on the poles each winter, and the teacher would have to pour water on it to release him. Boy, would he scream! He would also lay down on the ground and lap water from the rut around the merry-go-round, which would get lots of screams from the kids and certainly get the teacher's attention.

There were two outhouses, one for boys and one for girls, a Sears, Roebuck & Co. catalog in each for wiping paper. These buildings were placed way back on the lot, because you can just imagine how stinky they were when the weather was warm. And during the winter months, sitting in that cold, drafty, stinky place was not where you wanted to sit for very long! To be honest, it froze your behind.

The teacher had the little desks all in a row for grades one through eight. Each grade took a turn listening to her teach while the other grades did their studying, writing, or memory work. They started out the day by saying the Pledge of Allegiance and singing "God Bless America." With her little harmonica, the teacher would lead, and the kids sang as loud as they could, all off key. There was no talk of notes or scales. They just sang their little hearts out. By now, the fire was warming the room up, so the girls peeled off their long, brown, wet stockings and hung them on the clothesline. The boys sat in their wet pants, which actually steamed as they dried on their legs.

I watched Donnie doing homework after chores were done. We had twenty cows to milk, animals to feed, and other barn work. He would sit by the kerosene lantern and do what I thought to be very interesting writings with a paper and pencil. When I was about four years old, I begged to go with him and see what this "school" was all about.

Mother packed a lunch with a fried egg sandwich and cookie in our little lunchbox, and off I walked alongside my big brother, past Brown's farm and fields of tall corn and cows in the pasture. The state did not have kindergarten or preschool in those years, but the kind teacher let me sit in the corner and watch what was going on as long as I was as quiet as a mouse.

I loved sitting on my little chair and watching all this go on and did so for several weeks without making a sound. Then a CALAMITY happened! A new family moved into a vacant farmhouse and five more kids were to come to school! The teacher told me very kindly that I could not come anymore because they didn't have enough desks and had to use my little chair for one of the new kids. I was not registered, as I was not old enough to be coming to school. I had to go home.

You can just imagine how I took off walking that morning. I cried, I bellowed, I yelled, I screamed, walking the whole mile and a half home. A neighbor passed in his car and asked if he could help me, but I wanted the whole WORLD and GOD to know how mad I was and continued walking. The man drove to our farm and told my mother about the situation. Mother came running down the hill to see what the matter was. I was too sad to even tell. I cried for days.

The five new kids were not at all clean and brought lice to the school kids. We had to wash our hair with kerosene, and it burned our scalp like crazy. I hated them—all five of them! Why didn't they go back to where they came from? You know, they did. But by that time, I could legally go to first grade.

Walking to school, going right past Allen Brown's watermelon patch was just too tempting for Donnie and some of his friends. I must have been about six years old when the boys planned a late-night robbery. They were to meet at the abandoned house across the road from Brown's at 6:30 p.m. I listened secretly as they hatched this dangerous and exciting plan. So, when Donnie took off after chores, I followed quietly and was in the shack when the boys gathered.

"Who said *she* could come?"

"Send that twerp home!"

There really was no time to argue, the window of opportunity was closing. So, they pretended I wasn't even there.

Hunching down and quietly crossing the dark road, they tiptoed into the garden and found several big watermelons. As they ripped them from the vine, out of Brown's house came the maddest, loudest, monster dog, and Mr. Brown was right behind him. He was shooting his shotgun into the air. WHAM BAM! He was madder than a hornet, screaming and threatening to murder anyone he caught in his garden.

Murder? He was going to kill us? Oh boy, I should have stayed home. It was dark, and *Mother* was going to kill us when she found out. Faster than lightning, the boys turned around and ran right over me, crawling on my belly in the dirt. Only one watermelon made it safely to the old shack. By the time I limped back through the darkness and crawled through the door, the boys had cracked open the melon and were eating the red, juicy fruit. They did share some with me.

That was my first and only robbery. It wasn't that good, and my dress was a mess. I got into trouble with both Dad and Mom. *Big* trouble!

All-Star Wrestling

By Tamara McClintock

When I was in elementary school, I didn't consider myself different from other little girls. My favorite Christmas presents always included new clothes for my Barbie dolls, and I loved accessorizing each outfit. And, of course, I had to have the Ken doll, so Barbie could have a boyfriend—even though he wasn't anatomically correct.

Though I had the same interests as other girls my age, there was one activity none of my girlfriends shared. On Saturday mornings at 10:00 a.m., I would sit on the living room sofa with Dad and watch *All-Star Wrestling*. My sister and mother weren't interested in the show, so they always found another place to go during that time. Because my parents didn't have sons, I felt like I could keep Dad company during this "guy" activity.

I must admit I wasn't that interested in watching wrestling matches at first, but eventually, the show grew on me. Doug Gilbert and Rene Goulet were my favorite wrestlers. It was astounding to see that tag team fly over the turnbuckles like circus performers. At some point, the Crusher would charge into the room and say in graphic terms how he was going to demolish all his opponents, and the crowd would boo and get riled. Marty O'Neil— this short, balding commentator—would then shake his head and say, "Oh man, oh man, oh man . . ." like he was afraid the Crusher would sock *him*. Then there was Kenny Jay. No matter who Kenny Jay was up against, you knew he would lose. That was a given. I remember feeling sorry for guys like him. I thought maybe they needed to find another line of work.

The "Wrestling Champion of the World" was Verne Gagne. This guy embodied the traditional good-guy qualities of humility and fighting fair. He truly utilized wrestling moves as opposed to just beating the crap out of an opponent. I would cheer him on and relish each of his victories.

After the weekend, it was back to my elementary school. Girls were required to wear dresses or skirts to school at that time. In winter, when recess came around, we'd have to put pants on under our dresses to avoid getting frostbitten legs. It was very uncomfortable.

One day when I was in fourth grade, a bully who had been pestering me during recess suddenly shoved me into a snowbank. My bottom got soaking wet, and I knew I would have to sit in class the rest of the afternoon feeling all cold and clammy with wet underwear. As he laughed at my predicament, the many hours I'd watched of *All-Star Wrestling* flooded my brain. I charged at him and took him down so that he landed on his stomach. Swiftly, I jumped on his back and shoved his face into the snow. Amazed and confused—and blowing snow from his nose—he threatened to tell the principal. I panicked as I thought about how disappointed my parents would be if I got in trouble at school, and with false bravado, I warned him, "If you tell on me, I'll beat you up after school!" Mind you, I didn't know if I really could carry out that threat, but I hoped it wouldn't come to that.

Back in the classroom, I was waiting for the proverbial axe to fall, but nothing happened. The bully never ratted me out! In fact, when Valentine's Day came around the month after, he gave me a box of chocolates as a peace offering. Figure that one out!

Looking back, this incident carries with it a sense of satisfaction. The women characters in television and movies during my elementary school years were helpless and subservient. Where did I get the idea that, instead of hoping a guy would come to my rescue, I could deal with the problem myself? My wrestling win obviously made an impression, since no boy ever messed with me on the playground again.

When I was in the fifth grade, I begged my dad to take me to see a live wrestling event. Tired of my pestering, he revealed to me that all of these matches were staged, the outcomes planned ahead of time. I was shocked! Verne Gagne wasn't *really* the wrestling champion of the world? Kenny Jay made his living by *purposely* losing each match? The Crusher was just memorizing lines like an actor on the stage? I felt disillusioned, betrayed.

The next Saturday, at 10:00 a.m., the wrestlers were once again energizing the TV crowd, but I was in my bedroom, happily accessorizing my Barbie dolls' outfits.

THE GIFT

By Faye Schreder

It has been almost a year since any new toys came into the house. The shiny pages of the Montgomery Ward catalog have long been rumpled and tattered by the wistful little fingers of Santa's faithful as they hope for a bountiful Christmas. Those of us to whom Santa is no longer real know that Mama, in spite of her meager resources in these war years, will modestly provide one or two "perfect" gifts for each child in her large family. When we awaken on Christmas morning, we'll find the unwrapped gifts in a joyful array under the tree.

Our small house offers few places to hide parcels until Santa's visit, but it is a long wait from year to year and as the holiday nears, and we children are tempted to snoop in hopes of getting a glimpse of what's to come.

One evening, about ten days before the holiday, we are home alone when nine-year-old Jerry muses with a glint in his eye, "I wonder where Mama hid the Christmas presents!"

Wide-eyed, we stare at each other in silence until Bernice finally voices our thoughts. "Should we look for them?" Since our parents are away and the little ones asleep, conditions are ideal for a search.

Jean, the eldest and the one in charge, warns, "If they come home and catch us, we'll be in trouble!"

"Well, maybe we could just peek in a few places," Dick offers by way of compromise. We look in Mama's closet and under their bed but find nothing. It's just enough to sharpen our curiosity and dull our consciences. The search is on!

Dick is deep in thought for a few moments, then says, "Well, I guess we'll just have to check out her favorite hiding places!" He pulls up a wooden kitchen chair, climbs onto it, and stands on his tiptoes, reaching for the ceiling. "I still can't reach," he says.

"Here," Dennis offers, brandishing the broom, "Use this!" Dick grabs the broom handle, shoves it against the trap door, lifts it slightly, and guides it aside, revealing a two-foot-wide, square opening in the ceiling. A rush of frigid air descends from its inky blackness.

"We'll have to boost somebody up, somebody not too heavy!" Dick says. "Who wants to go?"

"I do! Please let me, please!" I beg to be chosen for this important job. I just turned seven, and it's my first year being included in this grown-up secret.

"Come on, then," Dick says, "I'll boost you up." I climb onto the chair beside him and step into his cupped hands. "Here you go!" he says as I lunge through the opening and hang on with my elbows. One last push, and I scramble into the darkness, pulling my skinny legs up after me.

Shivering from excitement as well as the cold air, I hunch on the floor joists, and for the first time, I'm not afraid of the dark! The keen smell of home-sawed lumber tweaks my nostrils from rafters so low I can hardly stand upright in the center. "Remember to stay on the beams so you don't fall through the ceiling," Jean calls to me, knowing that as the eldest, she is responsible for whatever happens when our parents are away.

"I know," I answer, shoving last summer's canning jars out of the way. It's my job to grope through the darkness, feeling for the packages, then strike a kitchen match for light and report the contents to my siblings below. One by one, I pull items from shopping bags randomly tossed onto the joists. I pull out a handmade dress and coat for a doll, a red toy tractor, coloring books and crayons, a jump rope, a flashlight, and warm mittens. There are also things for my older sisters: perfume, a diary, hair ribbons, and socks. As I call out the contents to my audience below, they debate the likely recipient of each item.

"You need to come down right now, Faye!" As Jean calls to me, I happen upon one last package. It's a small, glass globe holding figures of a little girl and a puppy. It's filled with liquid, and when inverted and then turned upright, snowflakes gently swirl around the figures. It's the prettiest thing I've ever seen! Forgetting about the cold, I keep turning it until the flame of the match I'm holding touches my fingers. I light another and play with the toy until that match burns out.

Finally, I return the globe to the bag and crawl back toward the shaft of light. Sliding on my belly over to the opening, I drop my feet onto my brother's waiting hands, and he lowers me into the room. He pushes the trapdoor back into place, and we all promise each other we won't tell our parents, no matter what! I hardly dare to hope the snowflake girl is for me, and I fall asleep with snowflakes swirling in my dreams.

At last, Christmas morning is here, but the globe is not under the tree! Later, my mother shows me the once magical gift. "This was for you, Faye," she tells me. "But it got so cold in the attic that the water in the globe froze and broke the glass."

How could such a pretty thing become so dull and lifeless? The snowflakes are gone, and the figures are bare and drab in the broken globe. "Thank you, Mama." I try in vain to put the pieces together and recapture its beauty, and finally set it aside.

I wish I had told Mama I saw it when it was beautiful, but I didn't. She didn't know that for a few brief moments in that cold attic, her special gift had already made me happy.

(Hide and) Seek

By Mardi Knudson

Giggle, giggle, shriek, laugh,
Wandering looking for their path

In the cupboard, under the bed.
I am the witch with the pointed head
They are the goblins I should dread.

Behind the door hints of tap tapping
Just one more game, then promises of napping.

I grab, feign a miss
When found, get a kiss.

"Where are you?" I query at each game start
Seeking three young grandkids
Finding love in my heart.

CATCHING THE TRAIN AT HOWRAH STATION

By Lalita Subrahmanyan

When I reminisce about my family—my mother, father, and two twin brothers—I am touched by the devotion and fierce loyalty of Amma, my mother, to her husband and children; the profound sense of duty and responsibility (dharma) of Appa, my father, the patriarch; and the implicit, unshakeable trust we, as children, had in our parents' ability to guide and protect us from all harm. Serious as that may sound, we had our moments! One of them was our experience of boarding the train from Howrah Station in Kolkata to Chennai for our summer holidays.

Every other April, the hottest month of the year, Appa could be seen making second-class sleeper reservations, sometimes for all five of us but often just for my mother and us children. Amma's task was to pack metal trunks with clothes and gifts; canvas holdalls with travel mattresses, sheets, and pillows; and bags with snacks and water for the forty-hour train ride. I would always pack my favorite reading materials and a writing journal that had earned me the unflattering nickname of Della Street, Perry Mason's secretary in an old English mystery series by Erle Stanley Gardner.

We always took a short train trip to Kolkata, to the home of one of my father's dearest friends, the day before we left for Chennai. My father wanted us to arrive in time to catch the train to Chennai the next day and, more importantly, spend some time with Mama (Uncle) and Mami (Aunty).

After we had parked ourselves in the spare bedroom of their spacious home, I would spend my time sitting among our luggage reading Enid Blyton stories and imagining myself camping in a little caravan like the Famous Five, having adventures, and solving mysteries.

Mama and Appa would be in the drawing room chatting about Mama's shipping business and Appa's work. Amma would attempt to spend a little time with Mami in the kitchen but would inevitably be interrupted by some commotion that resulted in her having to chase after my excited brothers, sometimes calling out to me to help her. You see, ever since my brothers were born when I was five years old, I had been her childcare assistant when the nanny was not present.

The next day, after a sumptuous breakfast and lunch, we would pack up our belongings, along with the delicious chapatis and *aloo sabzi* Mami and her cook had prepared for our journey, to begin the long wait for Mama to come home from work to take us to the station. He was always late!

After several worried and stern phone calls from Mami and calm excuses from Mama, his little Fiat car would appear at the door and all of us would pile in, with the luggage crammed into the trunk, the bags on our laps, and my brothers wedged between my mother and me.

Then would begin the exciting car ride to the station: the roar of a Fiat, sometimes without its muffler; the rattling of the luggage in the trunk, the door of which was held down by a cord; the swerves at every turn; and the sudden brakes to avoid a cow, a rickshaw, or a wayward driver suddenly appearing from a side street. It was nerve-racking and adventurous, sentiments I know my father, my brothers, and I enjoyed a whole lot more than my mother!

Upon arriving at the station, Mama would drop us off at the entrance and rush off to park his car. With the remarkable speed of years of practice, my father would get a porter to pick up the trunks and holdalls, and we would run down the platform as if all the leopards in the Kolkata Zoo were after us. It was quite a sight, although not unusual, because there were several other families running along as well.

My father would run behind the porter, holding some bags; my mother would follow, grasping one of my brothers with each of her hands in a vicelike grip; and I would follow, carrying the lighter bags, yelling at my brothers to stop trying to yank Amma's arms out of her sockets just so they could examine other matters of interest at the station.

Mama would catch up, huffing and puffing behind us. Suddenly, to our horror, we would see the guard waving a flag and blowing his whistle.

More than once, I had even seen the train slowly start to move out of the station. Turning around in dismay, I would see Mama wave at my father to carry on while he stopped. Calmly, he would go up to the guard and whisper something to him. "Oh, the guards are my friends," he would say if we ever asked him about it.

Quite miraculously, with a huge lurch and clatter, the train would come to a stop, and we would reach our reserved car. After that, it was a scramble getting into the car and finding our seats. Only then did we let out the breaths we had been holding for so long. Soon the train would leave. I would help my mother put away the luggage by making sure my brothers didn't run off to the door on the other side. My father would pay the porter and disappear, only to be seen standing at the door, leaning out and waving goodbye to his buddy.

We were off to Chennai to see our grandparents!

WHY WE EAT LEFSE WITH OUR FINGERS

By Mardi Knudson

Come gather round the fireplace, Grandchildren, and I will tell you the story of how Norwegians came to eat lefse with their fingers.

A part of who you are is called Norwegian. It is that red-blue part of your blood that flows through your veins and mixes with the other parts. The Norwegian part makes you very special, and we help that part of you stay special by feeding it lefse.

This story happened in a year long ago, in a time before your mother and father were born. Even before their mother and father were born.

The year was 1910. A nineteen-year-old girl named Olga Flatt came to this country, America, on a boat called the *Lusitania*, because her family wanted her to have a better life here. She came from a place called Over Halden, Norway. Olga was not much older than you, Grandchildren, and she traveled alone across the vast Atlantic Ocean. That ocean has so much water that the voyage took her four days.

Olga ended up in a place called Superior, Wisconsin, where she worked as a maid. There, she met your great-great grandfather—another young Norwegian. Together, they had a family, with seven Norwegian children. That is a lot of mouths to feed and food to prepare. Imagine setting nine plates and forks out on your table for three meals every day. *Uff da*. And those seven children were always hungry. It was expensive to keep feeding that many children. Not only that, but after they had their meal, they would have to wash all those dishes. This story is so old that there weren't even dishwashers back then. Those seven children had to wash the dishes by hand!

Sometimes the children would complain about having to wash so many dishes. Do you ever complain about having to put your plate and silverware in the dishwasher? Those Norwegian children had to carry the nine plates and forks to the sink filled with hot, soapy water. After washing that many dishes, their fingers would get all wrinkly and look like withered raisins from being in the water and scrubbing all that silverware and nine heavy plates.

Olga thought and thought about how to make life easier for her seven children. She needed something that didn't take many ingredients, because they didn't have much money. And she wanted there to be as little to clean up as possible. How was she going to feed seven hungry children and not use many dishes?

She thought back to her family in Norway and what her mother would feed their large family. Should she make lutefisk, cod soaked in lye? No, that fish was too smelly and wiggly! Should she make klubb, Norwegian potato dumplings. No, that uses too many dishes. Should she make fyrstekake? Norwegian cardamom-almond tart. No, the cream and cardamom are too expensive.

Her face crinkled into a happy smile. Of course, she would make lefse! Olga remembered the potato flatbread her mother would serve, eaten with fingers. Perfect, she reasoned. Now her seven prune-fingered, hungry children would have happy fingers and full stomachs when they made lefse.

You know lefse, Grandchildren. That is the potato tortilla we make for our special holidays. Olga gathered her seven hungry children and divulged her plan. She immediately had fourteen eager, helping hands.

They put peeled potatoes in a big pot of boiling water. When a fork poked into the soft tubers, they squeezed them through the metal ricer. In the drained pot, they added the riced potatoes, lard, salt, flour, and just enough cream to help the dough take shape. Seven stomachs were beginning to grumble. Now the children had to wait for the dough to cool. When it was just right, each child took a ball of chilled potato dough and gently pressed it flat in the palm of their hand. This soft disc was placed in the middle of a floured board. Then they took turns rolling the grooved rolling pin back and forth, back and forth, until they had a very thick circle. Next, they took a lefse stick and ever so carefully slid it under the flattened crepe, lifted it, and placed it on the hot griddle to fry. They turned it over once to get the brown spots on both sides. After the lefse was fried, it was stacked in tea towels to cool.

Then came the best part, the part that feeds our Norwegian blood. They cut the pieces of lefse in half, slathered on lots of butter, rolled the edges together, picked them up with their fingers, and ate them. *Yum.* They didn't care if butter dripped down their chins or made their fingers greasy, because the buttery flatbread treated their taste buds to a delicious, warm, potatoey flavor. Best of all, there were very few dishes to wash.

And that, my grandchildren, is how we came to eat lefse with our fingers. So little people, like yourselves, wouldn't get dishpan hands!

Olga Flatt and her seven children

THE RED MITTENS

By Faye Schreder

Winter had settled in! It was late November. The pond had frozen over, and snow covered the stubble in the cornfields. Running down the road to our country school in the mornings, I pulled my hands up into the sleeves of my coat to keep them warm because I had no mittens. My seventh birthday was coming up on Thanksgiving, and I was hoping to be surprised with a new pair.

My birthday finally came, but there were no mittens. Instead, Mama handed me a beautiful skein of red yarn. "This was left over from tying a quilt," she said. "Dick will knit you a pair of mittens."

"Red! My favorite color!" I shrieked, burying my fingers and nose in the downy softness. Turning to my older brother, I pestered, "When can you start my mittens?"

"As soon as the chores are finished this evening," he promised. At twelve years old, Dick was my protector and hero—the one who taught me to ride a bike, secrets about the Easter Bunny and Santa Claus, and how to read backward!

After supper, I raced through the darkness to the barn and tagged after my brother as he finished the evening chores. When all the animals were bedded down and the cows munching sweet clover hay, we left the warmth and stillness of the barn. Lantern swaying in Dick's hand, we tramped the short distance back to the house in the crunchy snow.

Once inside, before Dick could remove his boots, I thrust the knitting needles into his hands. "Hold on!" he laughed. "We'll get those mittens made!" He took his usual chair at the kitchen table and in the pale glow of the kerosene lamp began to cast on stitches. "This will take time," he told me. "I've never knit a pair of mittens before."

Forehead wrinkled in concentration, he counted the stitches, having an equal number on three needles. Within the fourth needle, he slowly began to make a cuff—knit two stitches, purl two. Soon his motions became rhythmic—needles click, yarn over, pull through. He was on his way!

Each evening, he picked up the needles and continued where he'd left off the night before. Each morning, I stretched out my hand, and he laid the unfinished mitten atop it to measure his progress. One morning, when only my fingertips were visible, he exclaimed, "I think I can finish this one tonight!" When I woke the following morning, one beautiful red mitten was waiting on the kitchen table.

Many mornings later, they were both finished! I gulped down my oatmeal and fidgeted while Mama braided my hair. She'd barely finished when I threw on my coat, cap, and overshoes and pulled on my brand-new mittens! On the way to school, I made snowballs and my hands stayed warm. Then, I waved and fluttered my arms like a cardinal in flight, watching those magical mittens light up the snowy countryside.

One cold morning a few days later, Uncle Ed stopped by with his horses and sleigh. A giant of a man with a full-moon face, he loved to tease and always called me Giggles. He stepped through the kitchen door, pulled off his leather mittens, and set them on the wood box. He stamped the snow from his boots and pushed his foggy glasses onto his forehead. When he noticed me, he clicked his tongue and poked me playfully with his chubby fingers. "You're gonna freeze out there today, Giggles!" he said. "It's twenty-four below!"

"Oh, I won't get cold!" I announced and proudly showed him my red mittens. He reached for them and teased, "These should fit me. I think I'll keep them!" and rammed his huge hand into the tiny mitten.

I watched in horror as the stitches gave way, and a great hole slowly spread between the thumb and palm of his hand. "Oops!" he said and hastily peeled the mitten from his hand. "Here you go, Giggles." A glance at Mama's angry face told him it was time for a quick retreat. He grabbed his own mittens and backed out the kitchen door.

After he left, Dick inspected the frayed mitten as a tear rolled down my cheek. "I think Mama can fix it," he consoled. "But there's no red yarn left."

Mama dug through her quilting supplies and pulled out a bit of brown yarn. "This will have to do," she said. First, she repaired the thumb, then started on the palm. I watched in dismay as she stitched in and out, in and out, until there was an ugly brown patch where the hole had been.

"Anyway, Faye," she said, smiling sadly, "they'll still keep your hands warm."

They did keep my hands warm, but from that moment, the magic was gone from my beautiful red mittens.

Uncle Ray

By Jerry Wellik

Uncle Ray
a farming man

carries little
scraps of paper

in pockets
wallet

poems riddles
jokes stories

quotes planting
tending harvesting

glorifying everything
on earth

Uncle Ray a ray
of golden sun

GRANDMA NORA

By Rachel Johnson

Grandma Nora was legendary in our family. She had beautiful, silvery-white hair she wore in a puffy French roll. She was bright, beautiful, and vivacious. She was known to have a wicked sharp tongue, if provoked, and a lead foot on the accelerator. Grandma Nora always moved full steam ahead. She put her all into everything she did.

Grandma Nora entertained her grandchildren, great-grandchildren, and even one great-great-grandchild with her exuberance and imagination. One time, as Grandpa Frank and I were watching her play with my daughter in the backyard, Grandpa Frank said, "I think she would bust a gut if she couldn't make those kids happy!" We both laughed a little, knowing it was true. If guts could bust, her guts would have long since been spilled all over the backyard.

Grandma Nora taught me a mastery of all things superstitious. I learned why and how to throw salt over my left shoulder, never to break a mirror, never to cross a black cat's path, and walking under a ladder was never to be done. If my palm itched, I was to come into money, and if my nose itched, I was going to kiss a fool. If my ears rang, someone was talking badly about me, and if I got a shiver, it meant someone was walking over my grave.

Grandma Nora gave me all sorts of sage advice. The topmost thing not to do was to marry someone a lot older than you. They would not like to dance, she told me. (Grandma Nora loved to dance—Grandpa Frank, not so much.) Grandma Nora's claim to fame was that she had danced with Lawrence Welk.

Grandma Nora always said I was the spitting image of her mother, Louise Eckardt. Louise did not like her picture taken, so there were only a few photos of her. But, every time we got together, we would go in Grandma's bedroom in an almost vain attempt to find a picture of her mother as proof. The pictures we did find were taken when she was older. I had a very hard time imagining I looked like her, much less a spitting image. But Grandma Nora persisted, so I knew it was true.

Grandma Nora had a twinkle in her eyes, especially if she was going to pull a trick on Grandpa Frank. One time when we vacationed in the mountains, Grandma Nora picked up some snow and made it into a snowball. I knew by the look in her eye that she was going to throw it at Grandpa Frank. I took a picture of her just before she let it fly—at Grandpa Frank.

My siblings and I went on many camping vacations with Grandma Nora and Grandpa Frank. We played the "Fire up" game while riding in the car. It was the most fun! We kids would yell, "Fire up" multiple times. (Three kids yelling "Fire up" in a small car made quite the racket.) Soon Grandma Nora would say, "If you do that one more time, I am going to sit on the roof of the car." Grandpa Frank would then yell, "Fire up" as loud as he could, at which point Grandpa Frank and us kids would dissolve into gales of giggles.

Grandma Nora liked the color pink. She unleashed her pink passion in an ultra-small bathroom. The walls were pink. Her decorations were pink. The toilet seat, one of those squishy foam ones, was pink. The lights were the old-fashioned fluorescent bulbs. When you turned them on, there was a metallic clink sound that for all the world sounded like "pink, pink, pink." Next, the two bulbs, one on each side of the mirror, would spring to life in little flashes. (Think strobe lights.) Every little fluorescent flash would show a pink peek at what was to come. When the fluorescent lights finally stopped flashing, there it was in all its glory—Grandma Nora's Pepto-Bismol pink bathroom. That pink bathroom was Grandma Nora's decorating zenith. She loved that bathroom.

Grandma Nora, as I said before, always persisted with whatever she got into her head she was going to do. She lived with Grandpa Frank, so her persistence was mostly focused on him. Grandpa Frank was often in the house with Grandma Nora, which was not always a good thing. So, he put a woodshop in an extra garage in the backyard. Grandma Nora soon found that walking with her bad leg to the backyard to talk to Grandpa Frank was not to her liking. (And she walked back there a lot.) So, first she got two walkie-talkies. She put one in the house and one in Grandpa's woodshop. But, it wasn't like a phone, so he did not know when she wanted him. Instead, she had a new phone line installed in the woodshop. One day when I was in the woodshop with Grandpa Frank, I heard the phone ring and ring. I thought Grandpa had not heard the phone, so I told him the phone was ringing. He said, "I know," and continued working. Not five minutes later, we heard Grandma Nora's dulcet tones shouting, "Frank. Fraaaank. FRANK!" Every time she said his name, her voice got louder, which meant she was on her way. Sure enough, seconds later, Grandma Nora burst into the woodshop. Grandma Nora had persisted again. Grandpa Frank sighed. I stifled a giggle.

We had coffee parties with real coffee in the cups mixed liberally with cream and sugar. We had New Year's Eve parties with 7-Up in wine glasses, complete with pointed hats and noisemakers. We even watched the glittering ball drop at midnight. (When I learned to tell time, I realized it was really 9:00 p.m. I never told Grandma. I didn't want to spoil her fun.)

Grandma Nora was bigger than life to generations of grandchildren, great-grandchildren, and one great-great grandchild. Her sense of fun was legendary. Her energy should have been bottled. I believe every child should have a Grandma Nora. We just got very, very lucky.

PAWS

By Elena Bookstrom White

The lion's paws under Grandma's table
Were solid—still are. They hover
On wheels over carpet patterns.
Back then, Grandma boasted
Of the worn path around the table,
Danced into the rug by miles of turning,
Hambos and waltzes, schottisches and polkas
Whirling by the cranked-up Victrola,
A rug danced down to bare tan threads.

Grandma Lisa and her girls did that.
We added play traffic of our own.
My cousin and I crossed the circling path
And played down low by the big brown paws,
Hidden under the heavy canopy.

What games and secrets?
Jacks outside the curled-back rug;
But underneath, family dramas,
Veiled by Grandma's tablecloth.
A safe home, solid;
The claws dark and polished,
Clean as everything in Grandma's house.
You could stretch your hand
Around a rounded paw
and hold it strong.

Now those paws
Are home still—in my home,
Far from 829 South Penn.
And when I clean so seldomly,
I get down close to the heavy claw feet,
Nicked old paws suspended
Over dust bunnies
And memories.

A Family's Influence—My Sisters

By Jean Eulberg-Steffenson

"Quiet," she whispered, "and remember the third step creaks!" We quietly and slowly moved up the staircase. She turned the knob with a very slight movement. The door barely opened, and we heard a loud crash—brooms and pans that had been placed against the door fell. Suddenly, our parents came running toward us, screaming, with brooms and a belt. My sister, three and a half years older, had gone first. Her longer legs flew up the stairs and into bed. I followed less quickly and got hit a few times. She claims I was just too slow! We crawled into our beds and pulled the covers up as our dad whipped a belt across. They were both still screaming at us about our late return.

They finally left, and we started laughing at the image of them waiting for their booby trap to go off so they could chase us, attack with a broom and belt, and holler at us. We laughed ourselves to sleep. Our crime was staying out late and creating thoughts in their minds of wild behaviors. Where had we been? Riding around the area in a car with her friends, laughing and joking. We were not drinking or doing anything wrong, but their minds went wild with the late hour.

This sister, Pat, influenced me frequently and sometimes led me to trouble, or I had to help her out of trouble! We had had not lived in this town for more a year. The boys flocked to her like dogs smelling a steak. She was very good-looking and had a great sense of humor. We had moved to Preston the past fall. My sister was a junior, and the boys were thrilled to have this new girl. I was only "Pat's younger sister." The girls in my class had trouble accepting a new girl. My sister felt bad and would often include me on her adventures. She introduced me to smoking. She trotted us off to a hardware store where a young, rather pale, thin man who was infatuated with her was working for his dad. We went to the back and shared a cigarette while we joked. She did not have an interest in him but just in a free cigarette! Ha!

The hot summer nights allowed us to sleep outside to stay cool. Sometimes, we would have a friend over. We laid our blankets down, played music and danced to it, and shared a cigarette that had been stolen from my mom or dad. One night, some of my sister's guy friends heard we were sleeping outside. They stopped by, and my parents heard them. That was the end of our sleeping outside. We were idiots though. I can remember us walking down the highway in the middle of the night and lying down on the highway lines to see how much longer they were than our bodies! A fast-moving car or truck would have killed us.

We were lucky. On Wednesday nights throughout the summer, a nearby town had dances for the teens in their roller-skating building. It was a highlight for all of us. At the beginning of the dance, the guys walked around the roller-skating circle, and the girls danced in the middle, except for a few brave couples who danced together. Toward the end, there were many more couples dancing. I often hitched a ride with my sister and her friends. One night, as we arrived back in town, they grabbed a watermelon that had been left outside by a store. We took it with us in the car. We drove up a steep, curvy hill that led to our city swimming pool. We cracked open the watermelon and shared it, and then we proceeded to climb the fence into the pool! We gave up and instead piled many of us into the car again and drove down the hill on a gravel road (which was mainly a hiking path). We bumped and hit our heads on the way down. Yes. We were idiots! When Pat left for college, I was very sad. She was only sixty miles away, but we didn't have our time together. Phone calls were rarely done then due to the expense. However, one weekend, I was able to stay with her at the college. She was at La Crosse. At first, she'd been in a private girls' college, but she couldn't handle it and transferred to La Crosse State. She was at La Crosse when I visited. All the young women were excited about the evening. La Crosse was a *big* bar and party town. Pat had a plan since I was not yet eighteen. We looked enough alike that I would take her license after she got in using the license. Well, for some odd reason, the bouncer didn't believe there were two Pat Eulbergs, and we were both kicked out! Obviously, this was not the best thought out plan.

I had two older sisters, with only one year between them. Susan was exactly what every teacher wanted for a student. Even though she had been in Preston for only a year when she graduated, she was salutatorian of her class. She frequently read. She was generally obedient and followed the rules. She felt overshadowed by Pat since she didn't have the guys chasing her. Although the teachers all would rather have Susan! She has a good sense of humor, and we all laughed a lot. On Saturday mornings, all of us would watch *American Bandstand*. We would sing loudly and dance. My mother, being exasperated with all of us, would come into the family room. We'd form a circle around her and sing, "Mary, Mary where are you going to?" Her name was Mary, and she just shook her head at us. My two younger sisters were two and a half years younger and six and a half years younger than me. I frequently took the youngest with me places. However, I usually followed the advice and actions of my sister, Pat, which was not always wise! I still feel close to all my sisters.

When I was diagnosed with triple-negative breast cancer a year ago, the two oldest called me almost daily. They sent flowers after each chemo treatment. None of my sisters drive very much, except for Pat. They all live in Southern Minnesota. So, it is usually up to me to drive to down there, which isn't always easy with my health this year and the increased traffic in the cities. My sister Pat moved to Florida from Wisconsin almost ten years ago. There have been a few years that I only see her once a year, but we frequently talk. Unlike phone calls years ago, we don't have to worry about the price. No matter what, all my sisters, even when they got me in trouble, have been a blessing in my life.

My Mother in the Kitchen

By Patsy Magelssen

Angeline Parkin was not of the gourmet category that I can remember. She was the oldest of four children and had lost her mother when she was eight and so had to help raise her three younger Italian siblings. I know she didn't own a cookbook, and even if she did, she wouldn't have stooped to following it.

Her cookies had a basic scoop, stir, and taste process. "All recipes are the same; you just add raisins. If they are raisin cookies, add peanut butter; if it's a peanut butter cookie, add a jelly blob for Christmas treats," she said proudly, knowing she had figured out a cooking secret.

She always had a pot of something red cooking, for most dishes contained tomatoes. Her spaghetti sauce was an absolute secret taken with her to heaven. It was wonderful, but you never knew if she had snuck in a few red-hot peppers until you swallowed, gasped, and grabbed for your water glass. You learned to ask, and she would never admit beforehand, but she had a certain smile and twinkle when she said, "It's *real* good!" Watch out. The more pronounced the *real*, the smaller first bite I took.

She had a small pressure-cooker pot, and into that went a piece of meat, be it squirrel, venison, beef, or a slab of pork (or maybe a cat or goat). The little round clock-type gauge thing on the top measured the degrees or pressure, and when it reached a certain point, a small knob sputtered and stream shot out of it. She then turned it off, let it cool down, and added every kind of vegetable that was sitting in the bottom of the refrigerator—plus tomatoes. Then she started it up again for about five minutes.

The trick was to watch that needle and be sure to turn it off or turn down the heat. One day, in about 1953, when we lived on Sheridan Avenue, she got careless and was most likely off crocheting (which was her real love in life) and forgot about her pot on the stove.

The steam was shooting halfway up to the ceiling, and a squealing, squeaking noise emitted from the pot's belly. The needle was way to the right-hand edge of its circumference, and just as I walked through the back door from school, all hell let loose!

I thought Japan had just bombed us again! The kettle exploded, sending the cover straight up through the plaster ceiling into the attic. Tomatoes hung in long, thick globs from the area around the hole, but the carrots and potatoes started falling *plop . . . plop . . . plop* to the floor, right after the ham bone.

Smokey, our black cocker spaniel, came rushing through the kitchen door. To his delight, supper had arrived at just his height—the floor. He grabbed that ham bone, burning his mouth and yapping and barking, his feet burning on the boiling goo. Mother had a broom by now and was hitting the dog to get back her supper meat.

My dad appeared in the doorway and just stood there numbly, looking at the twelve-inch hole in the ceiling and shaking his head. He couldn't even yell or curse—for several minutes.

Plaster covered the stove, sink, and floor, and Mom was crying about her wonderful pressure cooker and her lost supper. We never did get another cooker, but forty years later, I visited the people now owning that house, and sure enough, there in the ceiling above the stove was a round patch where Father had patched it up.

The lady living there chuckled when I told her how it came to be.

MY FAMILY

By Mary Lou Lenz

My Dad was mostly German, and my Mom was mostly Irish. I like to say that from St Patrick's Day on, I am Irish. This makes sense because in German, *lenz* means *spring*, and from the holidays on, I am German mostly, because of the stollen and lebkuchen and those unique German nutcrackers.

We didn't see as much of my dad's family because they lived in Watertown, Wisconsin, and we in La Crosse, Wisconsin, but since my Dad had a free pass as a ticket agent on the Milwaukee Road, we saw them often enough for them to have a big influence on my childhood. When we visited, I loved exploring their house. We stayed in an unfinished attic that had a big bed in it, and when not napping, I could look at my grandpa's painting materials and try on his protective paper caps (he even let me keep one) or choose which balls to play with from a big container. I loved watching my grandparents together. Grandma and Grandpa often danced in the kitchen if a good song came on the radio. I loved sitting with my grandpa in his favorite chair, talking to his canary, and sometimes, if lucky, listening to a story he would read to me. In this house, I sadly learned about the Second World War when my favorite uncle had come home earlier with something the adults called "shell shock." In hushed voices, they tried to explain to me why Uncle Bob was different. Their family was so sad about him, and neither my dad or my grandpa were the stereotypical German fathers who could not cry or show emotion. (My dad always cried at weddings.)

I remember, in particular, one story about my dad's mother, Louise. We were visiting, so there were about twelve people around the table enjoying Grandma's sauerbraten with gingersnaps. We were so involved with the delicious German food that it was suddenly quiet. Then my grandma piped up, "Great dinner, Louise, since it seems I am the only one who's going to say it!"

I think my mom was a little ashamed of my dad's being German because of the war with Germany. She didn't want him to make public his German roots, especially through his speech. He had a few German idioms, which I wish I could remember. But I do remember this one: "Mary Lou, make out the light." Then my mom would correct him. Even as a child, I wanted him to keep that way of talking because it reminded me of the love I had for my grandma in her long skirts, the nutcracker with which Grandpa would let me play, the bacon for every breakfast, and their close-knit family.

Maybe my dad got his love of music from his parents, because he and my mom both loved to sing around the house, and to this day, I can sing most of those songs, some of which I realized recently could be one hundred years old. I played and sang songs on my piano with names like "M is for the Million Things She Gave Me," "Mother," "Chickory Chick Cha La Cha La," and "Mares Eat Oats and Does Eat Oats, and Little Lambs Eat Ivy." Dad would also recite little ditties and adages of the day. I can remember him singing, "She'll have rings on her fingers and bells on her toes, and she will have music wherever she goes." I heard it so often, I believed it!

As I mentioned, my dad worked as a ticket agent for the Milwaukee Road all his life, and his job offered me some pleasant memories. I don't know how or why he was allowed to bring me to work with him (maybe my mom was having baby Jackie), but I could type on his typewriter and work his adding machine. My favorite memory was when he gave me some money to go to the train station restaurant. I was allowed to roam all over the large, two-story building, enjoying a level of freedom most children of today would envy. (I might add here that as I became older, I was also allowed to roller-skate anywhere I wanted, walk to the swimming pool about a mile from home, and, with a friend, hike Granddad Bluff a mile in the other direction.)

A lot of my dad's coworkers called him Nig. I never knew if it was because he would get a good tan in the summer, or if it was because he had so many friends among the porters, conductors, cooks, and waiters on the train. My first experiences with people of color were through these friendships when we traveled. Our hometown schools and churches were all white. There were a few families of color, but they lived in another part of town, so I was as happy as he seemed be to broaden my social circle.

Our family did have some sadness. When I was ten and my little brother was four, he died from a ruptured appendix. My mother never recovered from it, and it had a profound effect on our family—but I will write about this in a future paper. The sadness was somewhat countered by the happiness we had when we adopted a baby boy. But as a ten-year-old still grieving the loss of her little brother, I remember thinking, "You can't just replace a little brother like you would a family pet!"

Even though it was a "mixed marriage," meaning my dad was Lutheran and my mom was Catholic (but, as she liked to say, not a Catholic who was holier than the Pope, and certainly not one of those lace-curtain Irish), I suspect I grew up like most kids of my generation. We were expected to live by the Golden Rule; to not exhibit back-talk or talk against anyone, especially not the clergy; to be always truthful; and, above all else, to clean our plates, because "the poor little children in Africa would be happy to have that food." I remember being so scrupulous, I went to the local Catholic bookstore and asked for a book that would help me with a more thorough "Examination of Conscience," because I needed to find more sins for when I went to confession.

My dad died at age ninety-five, proving all that bacon and sausage was good for him. His burial was in the Catholic cemetery (by then he had switched to Catholicism), which butted right up to the train tracks of the Milwaukee Road (his former employer). As if we or he had planned it, a passenger train, blaring its presence, surprised us all at the burial. The family looked at each other and cried even harder. How fitting for a life so influenced by the trains and travel. All the rest of my life, when I hear a train whistle, I think of my dad and the influence he had on my life.

Kolacky in the Kitchen

By Jerry Wellik

Flour encircling her fingernails
enticing smells
of heavenly food
calling me home.

Thoughts and prayers
in the trinity of containers
cherry, prune, poppy seed
filling the holy center of bread.

Playing "peek" with the toddler
asking eternal questions;
"Where's your pupik?"
"Hiding behind the poppy seed?"

Thumbprints of dough
touched by the master's hand
may perpetual light be upon them.
Kolacky in the kitchen.

ABOUT ELLEN

By James Ellickson

If you were me, you would probably want to hear a few stories about Ellen. After more than fifty-five years of marriage, this is a good place to write some of those stories. So, from the beginning. I grew up as an only child. Yes, I had an older brother, Roger, but he was six and a half years older than me, and he left for the Marine Corps at age seventeen. But that's another story.

So, I grew up as an only child with very little contact with girls. Yes, there was my mom and my elderly aunts, but I mean girls my age. But that doesn't mean I wasn't interested in girls, because I really was.

In high school, I realized I needed to develop some experience talking to girls. At church (that's a good place to start), I got confirmed in the eighth grade, and a great thing happened. We went to a really big church in South Minneapolis, with over ten thousand members, and about four hundred of those members were in high school, having just been confirmed. So, the church did a great thing. They divided the four hundred kids into lots of small groups of kids, with an adult as a leader for each group. And no more than twelve people could be in any group. My group had mostly girls! This was my chance! I got to know all of them really well, and I went out on dates with most of them. They became my very good friends. And it was very safe place to meet girls. Life was good.

Next, I finished high school and went to college. I had freshman English class with Professor Paulson at 8:00 a.m. on Saturday mornings. Professor Paulson liked to organize his students alphabetically, so my last name being Ellickson, I was near the front. But I was interested in a girl who came in late and walked in front of me to get to the B's, for Bjorlie. (Never be late, be early.) I enjoyed watching her on Saturday mornings for the whole year. At the end of the spring semester, we wrote our final exam, and I left the classroom at the same time as this girl I was watching. I struck up a conversation in the hallway.

"Hi. How do you think you did on the exam?"

She answered, "Okay." And then she walked off. So, I had the whole summer to think about her and this first meeting.

I got a summer job at Northern States Power Company, working in the bill collections department. I would call up people and ask them when they were going to pay their overdue electric bills. The implied threat was that NSP would turn off their electricity if they didn't pay quickly. I learned how to be persuasive in that job.

Fall semester came, and I returned to college. It was a tradition at the college to have a picture directory of all the first-year students. I found a picture of the girl I liked, and I called her up and asked her out, just to get acquainted and to watch a (free) movie. We had a nice time.

During our second year, the college had another tradition called "Computer Dating Night." The idea was that by sophomore year, the students who were going to drop out of school had already done so, and the rest of us were fair game to be potential boyfriends. Here's how it worked. Remember this was the 1960s, and computers were all brand-new to everyone. The college got one of these brand-new computers, and the professors hid it somewhere. But the students got the idea that the computer, which was smarter than anyone, could solve our dating problems.

So, a student committee was formed, and they handed out paper surveys to anyone interested in a computer-assisted date. The students filled out their forms, and then they returned them to the committee. Somehow, the results were fed into the computer, which generated two long lists of names: first, a list of all the men, each with a number based upon their survey responses, and another list of the women, with each participant having a number.

Then the big night came when all the men lined up outside according to their numbers, and all the ladies lined up inside a building according to their numbers. Then, two by two, the couples walked through curtains and met each other—sometimes for the first time—like a computer-generated melding of numbers, like a well-choreographed, blind-date machine! Men and women would meet each other, make small talk, and try to figure out what to do for the rest of the evening.

Except for Jim and Ellen, who had been dating for many months by then, and everybody on campus already knew they were an "item." But then the computer matched them together! And who was going to argue with a computer?

The Ring

By Deb McAlister

A slender gold band,
Seven opals the color of summer sky and tranquil seas
Surrounded by tiny pearls,
So delicate,
Adorning these old hands
With arthritic knobs and wrinkles and brownish blotches,
Hands resembling my grandmother's hands
The way I remember them.
Not delicate, but strong and capable,
Digging in the dirt of her rose gardens,
Kneading dough for her cinnamon rolls,
Cutting cloth and sewing dresses for my sister and me.
I don't remember my grandmother wearing this ring
Given to her by a beloved aunt,
But one day she took it out of her jewel case and gave it to me,
Her first beloved granddaughter.
Now I wear it on my aging hands and think of her.

Sue—My Double Cousin and Friend

By Rachel Johnson

Sue is my double cousin. We share double DNA, and it shows. The first time we met was in the middle of a parking lot in New Hampshire. We had made plans to meet and spend a few days together going to see our Beede family home sites, a museum, and a historical society that had information on our ancestors.

Our families had both asked us if we were afraid to sleep in the same room as a cousin we had never met. Their thinking was that one or the other of us might be an axe murderess. We both replied that was not one of our worries.

We checked into the first motel for the night, got the keys, parked in front of the room door, and inserted the key, but the door was stuck. So, I hip-checked the door to get it unstuck. I hit the door so hard I almost flew into the room. I did not expect what I saw next. There in our room was a couple in bed. One was sleeping, the other in the process of sitting up after hearing the door open. As quickly as I had flown into the room, I left the room, slamming the door shut. I told Sue we needed to get another room and walked away. Sue followed as I said, "There is someone in there."

The next day, we got into Sue's car to go to Sandwich, New Hampshire. We were having such a nice time, we added a day to the trip. We got lost in New Hampshire and ended up in a Massachusetts cemetery. We checked the cemetery for Beedes, found none, and then left. Next, we found ourselves on a one-lane road with a picturesque bridge. I wanted a picture of the bridge. Since it was a one-lane road, there was a sign that said to honk when approaching the bridge so oncoming traffic would know we were on the other side of the bridge. Sue honked the horn the entire time I was framing the shot and taking the picture. It was the loudest picture I had ever taken in such a serene location.

We both had a devil-may-care attitude. We both talked a blue streak, and by the time we had seen all Sandwich, New Hampshire had to offer, the population knew we were the double cousins who had just met but could finish each other's sentences.

The last night of our vacation proved to resemble a Lucy and Ethel screwball comedy episode. I had a walking boot from a broken foot, so I could not drive. Sue had a neck problem that cropped up from time to time. That night was one of those times. I went to sleep quickly but woke up shortly after. I just knew something was wrong. I looked at Sue, and she was obviously in pain. Sue told me she could not hold her head up. I told her she should go to the hospital. She said she didn't want to ruin our trip. While I was sleeping, Sue had made a plan for the next day. She would drop me off at our next destination. She would stay in the car and recline her driver's seat. Since I had a boot and couldn't drive and Sue may not be able to drive, we would then be stranded in New Hampshire. I told Sue I did not think that was a good idea.

At that point, Sue went into the bathroom. I heard her say, "I am dizzy, Rachel." The bathroom was roughly the size of an outhouse, and the window the size of an outhouse window. The last time Sue had gotten dizzy in a bathroom, she had passed out, and the rescue crew had to extract her from her bathroom. If she passed out in this bathroom, they would have to knock down the wall. So I said, "Sue, I'm calling an ambulance. See, this is me calling an ambulance!"

By this time, it was 3:00 a.m. I concocted a crazy plan, which included involving our husbands. Sue called Bob, her husband, and I called Wayne, my husband. Wayne was in a campground in Maine. Wayne, who had never met Bob, had to pick up Bob at home in Clinton, Maine, and bring him to New Hampshire to pick up Sue's car. Then Bob could meet Sue at the hospital. Wayne and I would continue our trip.

It took quite a while for the ambulance to arrive. When the ambulance finally arrived, Sue was in more pain. The first thing they did was give Sue an injection to relieve the pain. That injection perked Sue up. When the ambulance crew was going to put a collar around Sue's neck, she said,

"No, let me do it. This has happened before. I know just what to do." I knew everything was going to be okay. Sue had taken charge.

Sue put the collar around her neck, got herself up, and put herself on the gurney. The last I saw of Sue that night, she was explaining to the ambulance crew that they had better have a lot of good pain medicine. The roads out of the neighborhood were very curvy and rough.

Sue got out of the hospital the same day she was brought in. They gave her pain medicine, told her to go see her regular doctor, and sent her home. Wayne and I went on to see the rest of the family sites in and around Sandwich and Tamworth, New Hampshire.

We arrived in Bar Harbor, Maine, two days after "the event." The first thing we did was go to visit Sue and Bob in Clinton, Maine. I wanted to make sure Sue was okay. Now you would think since Sue and I had just met that this would have been a very stressful event, but we worked together as a team, with a sense of humor and mutual respect for each other. We never got short or angry. We enjoyed each other's company and had the first meeting of a lifetime.

THE BIRTHDAY GREETING

By James Ellickson

Another war story. Any long-term relationship carries with it a collection of stories that are "classics." They can be pulled up from memory with only a word or two. My wife and I have the following example:

We were both in the military during the Vietnam War. Ellen was a Navy nurse stationed on the East Coast, taking care of wounded Marines. I was an Army private (a draftee) stationed on the West Coast. We were three time zones apart, we had been married two years, and we missed each other very much.

One day, I got up at 4:00 a.m. and went to the mess hall to work a twelve-hour "KP" shift. After work, in the late afternoon, I went outside to a telephone booth (remember telephone booths?) to make my call to Ellen.

When she answered, I said, "Hi. I didn't really have any reason to call you. I just wanted to talk a little at the end of the day."

There was a long pause.

Finally, she said, "You could have called to wish me a happy birthday!"

From that day forward, I never again missed her birthday.

AN UNEXPECTED MEETING

By Patricia Scott

On the hot afternoon of Thursday, August 23, 1973, I walked from the Arlington bus station to West Division Street, with my suitcase and guitar in hand. I had flown to Texas that morning to go to graduate school at the University of Texas at Arlington and had taken the bus from Dallas. I was overdressed, having arrived from Logan, Utah. Tired from the journey, and with the humidity, I was hoping I wouldn't have to walk too far. The sidewalks and road were bare of pedestrians and trees; next to the curb was sandy soil, rather than grass; the air was still.

Sure enough, on the other side of West Division Street (Highway 180), I saw the Oasis Motel described to me at the bus stop. I cautiously crossed the highway; fortunately, there was not a lot of traffic. I walked into the office, panting and sweating, and requested a room. The owner, a large, middle-aged man with sweat beading his forehead, looked me up and down and said he had no vacancies. Seeing my crestfallen look, he drove me to the Mayflower Motel farther down the highway.

At the Mayflower, a pleasant, slender, middle-aged man wearing tan slacks and a cream-colored polo shirt agreed to rent me a room for a week, since it was near the end of the tourist season. I paid in cash, took the key, and settled into my room on the first floor of a two-floor wing of rooms, all opening to the parking lot. The first thing I did was remove my jacket and turn on the air-conditioning, which felt delicious.

The next morning, wearing a tank top and jeans, I went directly to the office to get directions to various locations in town, such as restaurants, a grocery store, a church, and a laundromat. To my surprise, there was no sign of the dapper gentleman from the day before. Instead, there was a large, friendly, young man with a full head of coal-black hair, wearing baggy, navy blue, cotton Dickies work clothes. His name was George, and he obligingly answered my questions and offered to take me to the restaurant and the grocery store using his car.

That evening, as I was reading in my room, I heard an unexpected knock on the door. I peered cautiously outside and saw George, looking nervous and hopeful. "Would you like to go to a movie?" he asked.

"What's playing?" I asked. He turned around and walked back to the office, returning shortly with the titles. Since I had nothing better to do, I agreed to go with him. I kept looking at him out of the side of my eye to see if he was going to put the moves on me. Having dated a few college men, I was surprised he didn't try to get closer or hold my hand.

During the week, I found some student apartments in the newspaper, walked to one of them, and gave them my last $300 as a deposit. I set up a bank account to which my mother could send tuition money.

George made a quick weekend trip to Arkansas to visit family and re-new his driver's license. He was later than expected returning to the motel, and I got worried. When he finally appeared, I gave him a big hug. With his broad shoulders and muscular arms, it was a warm, reassuring embrace.

By the next Monday, I was broke, and I was sad because my mother had not been able to send money to the bank and because long-distance calls were expensive and I had just called her on Sunday. George took me out to breakfast. Seeing the long look on my face, he said, "For two cents, I'd ask you to marry me."

My stomach sank. I had recently broken up with an engineering stu-dent, and I had no interest in a serious romantic relationship. When we got to the restaurant, I said, "I can't marry you," and gave him several reasons why it wouldn't work out—a lot of them having to do with the differences in our backgrounds (me, the daughter of college-educated parents, versus George, who had dropped out of high school). Later, George told me he made those comments just to cheer me up, but my response made it more of a challenge.

George took me to the grocery store and helped me move into my new apartment, with a loan of crisp, clean motel bedding, before going to work. I was just cleaning up the supper dishes that first night when who should knock on my door but George. He gave me a story about being kicked out by his boss, so I allowed him to stay, and he never left.

The first time I had the chance to cook a meal for George, I asked him what kind of food he would like. His answer: "Mexican!" So I fixed a Mexican casserole from a recipe I got from a friend I'd met at a summer job in Evanston, Wyoming. George, who tended to say the first thing that came to mind (and still does), took one look at it and said, "What is this garbage?"

I said, "If you can do better, do so!" The next week, he presented me with homemade enchiladas, which, I had to admit, were superior to my casserole.

That Christmas, I brought George home to meet my parents. Despite their initial misgivings, he made a place in their hearts when he repaired their furnace during that cold Logan, Utah winter. In early June, he drove me to Arizona for a family reunion at my Grandma Watkins' place. We took our $75 Pontiac Bonneville, which floated along the highway. My eighty-four-year-old grandma, who had written to me, "Why don't you find a nice college boy?" loved him. She said, "If he were a little older, and I were a little younger, I'd give you a run for your money."

I had dropped out of the Graduate School of Social Work after a bad experience with my practicum assignment, so that summer, I was trying to get a job, without success. My parents wanted me to move back home to Logan. George's friend and mentor Mr. Faucher had a friend who was a drugstore manager, and he said he would help if we were married. My plan had been to finish my education before marriage, but the circumstances convinced me to move up the date. George was so excited that he called the justice of the peace right away, and we got in on July 3, 1974, "the day before the big bang." And I did get the job.

Over the next year, I became bored working as a drugstore clerk. I went back to graduate school with a change in majors, from social work to psychology. I was literally spending all my spare time studying, and George felt left out. In order to give me the time I needed, and to get some job training himself, he decided to join the Army.

Immediately after I graduated with my master's degree in psychology, since George was assigned to Ft. Carson, we moved to Colorado Springs, Colorado. Colorado Springs is a beautiful little town at the foot of the Rocky Mountains near Pikes Peak. As much as we liked it there, I could not find a professional position. George eventually found a job he liked in Denver, repairing ice machines, but he understood how important my career was to me and agreed to move across the country from Colorado to Minnesota when I was offered a job at the State Hospital in Brainerd. So we moved, with our firstborn in utero.

After forty-eight years of marriage, we have two adult children (both married), two grandchildren, and a miniature poodle mix.

I REMEMBER

By Ann Romanowsky

I remember summers at my grandparents' farm.
The dairy cow, Ginger, so gentle
The dairy bull so dangerous
Grandpa said he'd sooner
take his chances with a grizzly bear.

I remember the kitchen so hot
In August when tomatoes ripened.
Hotter yet with steam rising
From canning jars on the stove
Being readied for this year's crop.

A day's sweaty labors
Yielded gorgeous jars
All lined up on the shelf
Brimming with goodness
And self-satisfaction.

The Howard Johnson Family

By Martha Johnson

My parents grew up in Virginia, Minnesota, which is a small city in the northern part of the state. It is on what is referred to as "the Iron Range," which is actually three ranges where iron ore and taconite were mined. They were raised on opposite ends of the city—the north side and the south side. During the seventh grade, Howard E. Johnson and Mary Jean Hughes met for the first time. She used to sharpen his pencils, and it would always make him blush. He was much quieter than my outgoing mom.

They shared some of the same classes and social activities throughout the years but never dated on a one-on-one basis. Following his graduation from high school, he was drafted into the Army during World War II and was sent to serve the country in Europe. He was honorably discharged from the war upon the death of his father and returned home to his family.

It did not take long before my parents started dating and got engaged to be married. It was a small ceremony with only a justice of the peace and my mom's sister, Georgia, in attendance. They were now Mr. and Mrs. Howard Johnson. His name, Howard Johnson, made us laugh because we would book adjoining rooms at Howard Johnson Hotels that accommodated larger parties. In disbelief, the hotel staff always made him show his identification as proof of his name. They could not believe it! I'm certain we were the talk of the different hotels we stayed at!

Everyone always laughed, too, because if my parents had used my mom's last name, my father's name would have been Howard Hughes, the same one as the famous, multifaceted businessman who passed away in 1976. My mom frequently talked about how they took the 10:10 a.m. train to Winnipeg, Canada, for their honeymoon. After that, they moved to Minneapolis, Minnesota, to start their married lives together.

After seven years of marriage and many attempts at starting a family, they decided to adopt a child. Shortly after that, my mom finally got pregnant. They were thirty years old when they had their first child, Amy. By the time they were thirty-six years old, they'd had five more children! Grant was born after Amy, followed by me, Philip and Seth (aka the twins), and Sarah. My mom had her hands full and did not work outside the home once we children were born.

Even though there were now eight people in the family, we traveled up to Virginia quite frequently to visit the grandparents. It was one of my favorite things to do. We almost always went to Grandma and Grandpa Hughes's house first. There was usually a hot dish baking in the oven when we arrived. It was a casual, fun setting. Sometimes Grandma would take us to the park at the end of the block or to the store to buy some candy. She and everything she touched smelled like her Estée Lauder fragrance, even the cards and letters she sent us in the mail.

Grandpa Hughes slept downstairs in the basement on a big bed. My five siblings and I used to love climbing up onto his bed. It was so soft that we would sink into it. We also used to go outside into my grandpa's garden. He grew vegetables and flowers. We used to squeeze his snapdragon blossoms so that they looked like an open mouth. Before we were finished picking the ripe vegetables, we would pick some of the flowers. He would arrange them just how he wanted them, being mindful of mixing up different colors. It became a lovely bouquet for Grandma! She was always delighted when she received the garden flowers!

After visiting for a while at Grandma and Grandpa Hughes's house, we proceeded to the south side of Virginia, where my Grandma Johnson lived. Grandpa Johnson had died before we were even born. As soon as we walked through the door to her small house, we could smell the sweet aroma of freshly baked, homemade bread and sugar cookies. It was such a yummy smell! When we were at Grandma Johnson's, we had to be fairly quiet, use good manners, and help out as needed. It was much more formal than Grandma and Grandpa Hughes's place. We always had a meal there as well. By the time we got there, we were so full from Grandma Hughes's hot dish meal, but we still had to sit at the big table and eat. I remember having very wholesome meals there, though never a hot dish. The meals always included a meat, mashed potatoes, gravy, a vegetable, homemade buns, and *real* butter and milk. We used to kick each other's legs under the table, but we couldn't laugh. Grandma Johnson did not have a TV, nor did she believe in watching TV. There was no card playing either. She was Baptist, and she frequently read to us out of the Bible. My dad was not a big fan of her pushing religion on us. The last time I saw her, Grandma Johnson was sitting in her rocker, knee-high mukluks on. When she got older, she would say she was "waiting for the Lord to take her."

I'll never forget either of my grandmas or my Grandpa Hughes. Being with them are some of the best memories I have of my younger years. I still have a birthday card from my Grandma Hughes that has a fuzzy poodle on the front of it. Inside, there is a quarter taped to it. It's a special treasure I will keep forever.

Mary Jean Hughes Johnson

A Tribute to My Best Friend

By Cathy Peterson

At age three, my best friend was adopted. Her parents, who weren't able to have any children, were over the moon with joy about becoming her mom and dad. Sally Constance, who was nicknamed Connie for short, finally had her own family and knew she had been "handpicked." Her dad was a grain salesman, but he was also a talented musician in a band on nights and weekends, singing and playing the bass fiddle. Her mom was a music teacher and also taught piano lessons.

Connie would sit proudly in church each Sunday as her parents sang beautiful duets together. But it wasn't long before her mom became sick. Connie was only six when her adoptive mother died from throat cancer a couple weeks before Christmas that year. Her memories of the grief of that Christmas haunted her the rest of her life. Her dad courageously carried on his role of being her only parent.

Her father was strict, and he insisted music be an essential part of her upbringing. By the time she was seven, she was playing both the piano and the violin. She had been gifted with perfect pitch. Weekly lessons were a part of her regime, along with two hours of practice per day in addition to completing her assigned farm chores. This routine would last all through her high school years. She also was active in 4-H, learning to sew and cook. While she loved her music, Connie wanted to become a nurse after high school, even though she was awarded many music scholarships for college. By the time she was a senior in high school, she was the lead violinist in the Mankato State College Symphony, having studied there for the previous two years, riding the train alone from Wells to Mankato for weekly lessons. She certainly made her daddy proud.

But alas, she was not to become a nurse or follow through with her music career. Instead, she was pressured into getting married in 1951 by a man named Rex. (She later found out he'd been using her to keep from having to go fight in the war in Korea, because he insisted upon having children as soon as they could, too.) Before the tender age of twenty, she was the mother of two lively baby girls, helping with the farming of crops, and having sheep to raise. It was a tough life for this young mom. Of course, her dad was quite disappointed in her choices.

As the years went by, this auburn-haired mom was now raising three daughters, but Connie once again found her music and began playing her violin in church and to entertain various groups. She also unearthed her self-confidence and, although she was a stay-at-home mom, she began volunteering. She became a charter member of the Pink Ladies, who provided activities and monthly parties for the nursing home residents. She sewed clothes for her children, was diligent with meals being ready on time, and was involved in church with choir, being the substitute organist and serving as the Sunday School superintendent. She and Rex had also become involved in the local archery club. Everyone loved her bubbly personality and her vibrant laugh.

One day while she was at the grocery store, the owner approached her and asked her to enter a homemaker contest that was being sponsored by the Red Owl Company. All she had to do was write an essay. She hemmed and hawed but then decided, Why not? She submitted her inspiring essay. Within a couple of weeks, she was notified she was a finalist in the Mrs. Minnesota Pageant. She was elated! The pageant was held in August 1965, in Austin, Minnesota. The homemaker contest included cooking a full meal, baking and decorating a cake, washing and ironing, and having a talent to share. While she could have used playing the violin as her talent, she chose to use her talent in archery, where she could hit a ping-pong ball or the inside of a 45 record from fifteen yards away. Lo and behold, on a hot summer day, Connie won the title of Mrs. Minnesota 1965-66! News spread rapidly in their little town of twelve hundred, and Fulda became known as "the Home of Mrs. Minnesota." For the next few years, she spoke for countless groups and at colleges and traveled all over Minnesota. Her new wardrobe was also provided as a winning prize. She had always been a classy lady, but she was even more spectacular now, and the whole town was more than proud.

But the years married to Rex were more than tough, as he was an abusive and jealous man. How many times had he beaten her up and put bruises on her body? How many times had he kicked or slapped the children? Finally, when her daughters were in high school, she made the difficult decision to divorce him. This news angered Rex even more, and he threatened to kill them all, saying no lock would keep him out if he wanted to get into *his* house. Connie told the sheriff's office of his threats, and a red hotline phone was installed in her home in case of any emergencies or fear of more violence. But thankfully, Rex moved out.

Before long, Connie met a gentle man, a veterinarian named Bill. They became close, and together they moved to Las Vegas and married. He built a pet clinic, and Connie, now in this glamorous environment, became a violinist for Wayne Newton, playing second chair in his orchestra. Her daughters adored this new stepfather of theirs. Unfortunately, after twenty-five years of wedded bliss, Bill passed away from cancer.

Never to remarry, Connie was still an energetic soul involved in church choir, growing her red roses, writing poetry, and loving her grandchildren. For her eightieth birthday, her whole family gathered to celebrate eighty wonderful things about her and the ways they loved her. What a fabulous time that was! For several years, she was especially close to her middle daughter, who helped in numerous ways to complete genealogy searches and locate her biological family, one of the goals of her intriguing life, to know where she had come from.

Through all the years of excitement, abuse, and genealogy searching, my mom, who was always there for me, was my mentor, role model, and best friend. We shared everything and talked almost daily until Valentine's Day 2020, when she passed away unexpectedly in her assisted living facility in Las Vegas. I say that she was taken from earth on the day of love. I miss my best friend more than words can say, but I know she's with me forever.

FAMILY CHRISTMAS

By Patricia Scott

With snow crunching underfoot and frost nipping your nose in Logan, Utah, December seemed like a good time to take the train to Grandfather Watkins's house in Tucson, Arizona. The five of us would bundle up in the old Ford Fairlane and drive over the Wasatch Mountains to the depot in Ogden, a beautiful old building with colorful tiles arranged around a drinking fountain in the waiting room wall. It wasn't much warmer inside than out, as periodically, more people would come through the doors on the street side or the doors opening to the tracks, letting in cold air.

An announcement for the train to Bakersfield would come over the loudspeaker, and we would get up from the benches and head for the door. The train would blast its horn and roar up to the platform, squealing its brakes and letting off steam. "All aboard! All aboard!" the conductor would shout, and Dad would help my little sister up the steep steps leading into the passenger car. Then the train would huff and puff and start slowly down the track, gathering speed as it clicked and clacked on its way south.

Of course, we had to go to another car to find the toilet, and I found it particularly interesting to cross between cars, where the cold air came in through the accordioned sides and the metal floor of one car swayed against the floor of the next. My next favorite place was the Vista Dome, a car with a glass roof where we could watch the scenery go by, from the pines and mountains of Northern Utah, down through the colorful high deserts, to the flat desert plains.

After forty-nine and a half hours, sleeping in our seats, I am sure we were all happy to come back to earth in Tucson. Like sailors returned from the sea, our bodies swayed a little as we disembarked from the train. There, we were greeted by sandy ground, sparsely covered with tenacious grasses, mesquite, and sage brush. In contrast to daytime temperatures in the thirties and forties, we felt a blast of sixty-nine-degree heat. The hot, dry air felt good on my skin. Grandpa picked us up in the 1956 Chevy and drove us to their property on the edge of town, to the west of the highway. To the east, across the South Nogales highway (now Interstate 19), was the airport. To the south, there was a large, sandy lot with some giant metal structures like grain silos.

It was a magical place; enormous compared to our suburban lot, with a trailer park to the west, the gas station and convenience store in front, and the house behind on the east. In between, there were several outbuildings: a shower house with old-fashioned laundry tubs for the tenants; a ham radio shack for Grandpa, Dad, and his sons; and a small cabin that had been built before the house was. There were so many places to hide and play and pretend. We would run around all day in T-shirts and jeans. Our parents didn't worry we would wander off because there was no place to go. When the heat got to be too much, we would wander into the convenience store, and Grandpa would give us those old-fashioned popsicles on two sticks, until our mom put a stop to it.

The most challenging part of the visit was eating at the kitchen table with Grandma, Grandpa, and Uncle Nathan, who had cerebral palsy. He clumped up to the table with a walker, and he drooled as he ate. My dad and his brothers would get together with him and work on a Heathkit do-it-yourself radio with tubes.

One of my favorite day trips was to see the Arizona-Sonora Desert Museum, an outdoor adventure park similar to wildlife safaris in other states. As we walked along, we came to a large enclosure full of vultures, songbirds, and toucans. When we opened the outside door to come in, there were two large vultures sitting up high, keeping an eye on my mother, who was always thin. After a long day of sightseeing, we would return to the house very tired.

On the holiday itself, my Aunt Frances and her husband, Charles, would be there to help serve the feast. She would shred coleslaw for the salad, with the wonderful aroma of turkey and dressing cooking all day in the oven. I don't think Grandma baked her own pies, but we always had pumpkin, apple, and some other choices. We ate until we were sated. After dinner, we would all sit in the living room and enact a reader's theater with one of their many sets of books. You see, Grandma and Grandpa had been teachers in Missouri, but they had to move west when Grandma got tuberculosis. So, they had multiple copies of Shakespeare's plays, and each of us read a part (or more).

You can see why it was one of my favorite places to go.

PART

4

PASSAGES THROUGH LIFE'S JOURNEY

SCARY PREGNANCY

By Brad Busse

We were so excited when we found out we were pregnant! My wife and I were surprised yet pleased that we were expecting.

The pregnancy didn't go well. Shortly into it, we found out there were complications. My wife had what the doctors called an incompetent cervix, which meant she might deliver at any time. So, they performed a quick surgery, and all was well. But because of that, she had to be mostly bedridden for the last three months of her term. That meant she couldn't work, and that meant money troubles. However, we persevered.

Finally, the day came when she knew it was time. The week before, we had gone out for dinner, despite the weather. It was record cold in Tennessee, seventeen degrees below at one point, and there was snow! But we were prepared for anything.

The baby came, and things were good. Until we found out the little guy wasn't "pinking up." Seems he was a "meconium stain" baby. Usually, babies swallow an in vitro bowel movement. But our little guy inhaled it. Yep. He had baby poop coating his lungs.

When I found out, I rushed down to the nursery, determined to find out what was going on.

As I crossed the clearly marked line, a doctor told me, "No! You can't go past that line!" I apologized and felt very badly that I had screwed up. The doctor then, very gently, told me I had to stay on this side of the line.

He looked at me. Then he looked at the card on the bassinet that held my son. Then he asked, "Is your name Busse?"

"Yes."

"Is your dad's name William?"

"Yes."

A funny look came over his face. Then he smiled and said, "Your dad works for the American Lung Association?"

"Yes . . ."

Seems my dad, years before, had underwritten this particular doctor a scholarship to medical school through the American Lung Association. It seems he had become a specialist as a neonatal doctor who cared for troubled births. He stayed at my son's bedside for almost seventy-two hours.

End of the story, my son is now thirty-six. He has a bit of an inverted chest but is otherwise healthy. We now have two lovely grandsons, Noah and Evan.

Just goes to show you that a kindness sometimes takes a couple of decades to pay off.

THE FIRST TIME I WENT TO SCHOOL

By Rachel Johnson

The night before I started kindergarten, I was all abuzz with anticipation. I could hardly wait to go to bed, so it would be closer to getting up to go to kindergarten. I was also going to take the bus to kindergarten. I had watched the older kids in the neighborhood taking the bus forever. Now I would get to take the bus, too.

I went to bed better than usual, without the usual request to get another glass of water and then, of course, having to go to the bathroom. None of that this important first night before going to kindergarten, just a quick hug and kiss and right into bed.

I woke up at what I thought was the right time to go to school. It was still dark when I made my way downstairs to my parents' room. "Mom," I said, "I think it's time to get up to go to kindergarten."

"No, Rachel," she replied. "It's way too early. Go back to sleep." No way was I going back to sleep. I just knew I would be late for school. So I lay down in front of the heat grate in the living room, just outside my parents' bedroom door. That way, I would be warm when the heat went on, and I could be sure to get my mom up in time.

I waited for what seemed like forever and again woke my mom with my concerns about being late for school. My mom replied more forcefully, "Rachel, it is still dark. It is too early to go to school! Go back to sleep!" Again, I returned to the heating grate in front of my parents' room.

Finally, I could see that it was getting light outside. I started watching for the bus. That way, I knew there was no way I could miss it. I saw a bus drive by on the main road, but it did not turn down our street. *Could the bus not have been told I was going to kindergarten?* I thought.

Again, I returned to my parents' room. "Mom!" I said with urgency in my voice. "The bus drove by. But it must have forgotten me! It must be time to get up."

Again my mother said, "Rachel, it is not time to go to school. The school bus did not forget you. Go back to sleep."

At that point, I started wondering why my mom did not understand I was not going back to sleep. This was my *first day of kindergarten*! I was starting to think that it was never going to be time to get in the bus, that I was never going to get to kindergarten. I was starting to get upset.

Finally, after one hundred hours, my mom got out of bed. She said it was time to get ready to go to school. I got all dressed up in my prettiest brown plaid dress with white buttons and dressy shoes. I ran downstairs and got my hair combed. And then my mom said I could go out to the bus stop. The bus came, and I climbed aboard without even looking back. Finally, I thought, I was going to school.

CAN YOU HEAR THE OBOES COMING IN, EDDIE?

By J Vincent Hansen

For Ed Barthel, a city boy turned farmer.

In the middle of Beethoven's Symphony No.3
Sister Mary Margaret asked:

"Can you hear the oboes coming in, Eddie?"
"No Sister, I cannot hear them," Eddie replied.

Then Sister Mary Margaret said
she would play it over again
and this time Eddie to listen closer.

When Eddie told her
that he still could not hear the oboes entering
Sister Mary Margaret asked:
"What do you hear Eddie?"

Eddie replied, "I hear the cows coming in Sister."

Aware that Eddie's answer
housed neither sarcasm nor flippancy,
Sister Mary Margaret joined it then and there
to the earth under Eddie's nails
and what she deemed to be his innate goodness.

After some fertile seconds of silence,
in the conspiratorial voice of an accomplice,
Sister Mary Margaret leaned over
and whispered:

    "Go, Eddie; your cows are waiting
    and the God that I know will go with you."

County Fair

By Faye Schreder

On a late summer afternoon, Mama wiped her hands on her apron and surveyed the rows of jars that filled the kitchen like green soldiers standing at attention. "There," she said, "I've canned all the pickles we'll need for this winter!" She had to make enough for the entire year, because they took the place of fresh salads during the cold winter months.

Even after we canned all the pickles we needed, the vines still sprawled lazily in the garden, their yellow blossoms turning into more cucumbers the family could consume or give away.

When Daddy came home from work that evening, he decreed, "With all the people starving in the old country, we can't let those pickles go waste." It was decided that Carol and I, eight and nine years old respectively, would keep picking the cukes. Daddy would sell them in the evenings after work and then give us the money to spend at the Benton County Fair.

The next morning, we were temporarily excused from the hated job of wiping the breakfast dishes. Swinging a basket between us, we raced to the garden in the morning sunshine. We snapped the torpedo-shaped produce from the vines and plopped them into our basket in anticipation of overflowing coffers. Within days, however, the project grew tiresome, and we lost interest. Fresh green cukes were picked for supper each evening, the rest grew into fat, golden submarines, becoming a treat for the hogs in their pens. Carol and I were back to wiping breakfast dishes.

At last, it was county fair time, the highlight of our summer! For weeks, we children dreamed of merry-go-rounds and Ferris wheels as we made our way along the endless rows of vegetables in the family garden, pulling weeds and hoeing the caked earth. It was especially exciting this year, because Carol and I would be spending the day at the fair with no adult supervision. Daddy would drop us off on the way to his job at the Great Northern Car Shops and pick us up on his way home in the afternoon.

Mama cut thick slices of homemade bread and spread them with butter and fresh chokecherry jelly, wrapped them in wax paper, dropped the packet into a paper bag, and then tucked in a few warm oatmeal cookies. "Don't lose your lunch," she cautioned. "Here's your pickle money," she added, tying two quarters and a dime into the corner of a clean cotton handkerchief for each of us. "That should be enough for two rides each and an ice-cream cone." As we raced to the car, she cautioned, "Be good girls and don't waste your money on shills."

The morning air was cool when Daddy dropped us off at the fairgrounds. Instead of hustle and bustle, we were disappointed to find it quiet and sleepy. We wandered the midway, deserted except for an occasional carnival worker quietly tinkering on an engine. Tents were closed and concessions stands shuttered. We wandered past the drowsy tilt-a-whirl, its seats leaning drunkenly on the topsy-turvy floor, then past the festooned merry-go-round horses frozen rigidly in mid gallop. It was strange without all the sounds of the calliope, the shouts of the wheedling barkers, or the shrieks of the riders whirling in dizzy circles overhead. No multicolored lights blinked on the rides as generators sat idle, their fat electrical cables slithering from one attraction to another across the dusty sand.

We sauntered to the exhibit area, where the grass was thick and green, and stopped at the 4-H building. We looked at the exhibits, a breadboard in the shape of a pig, sawed by a schoolboy with the fine blade of a coping saw. There were cookies, three to a plate, and aprons and dresses made by the older girls, including our sisters, Jean and Bernice. We walked by the peach crates containing wilting carrots, kohlrabies, string beans, and tomatoes. The vegetable boxes reminded us of tedious days spent hoeing and weeding, so we moved on, taking a shortcut to the livestock buildings. It was cool in the barns, and peaceful, but we didn't stay long. After all, we didn't come to see farm animals. We could see them at home. We came for excitement! Rides! Noise! And we were anxious for the fun to begin.

By midmorning, our lunch bag was beginning to feel heavy, and the chokecherry jelly was soaking through, so we found a cool spot in the shade and ate an early lunch. The jelly was refreshingly tart on our tongues as we gobbled down our sandwiches. We thought Mama's oatmeal cookies with lots of raisins were the best in the world and ate every last crumb from the bottom of the bag. After eating, we untied our money from the corner of our hanky to check if it was still there. There it was—two quarters and a dime for each of us! We tied it again and shoved it to the bottom of our pockets, wondering how long we'd have to wait before spending it.

Before long, the breeze died and the humidity soared as the sizzling August sun crept directly overhead. Our stiff blue jeans, new for the school year, clung to our legs like canvas. Our new leather oxfords made our feet tired and hot after spending most of the summer barefoot. But we didn't care. At last, we were seeing some action! Churning rides, flashing lights, blaring music!

It was a heady experience, not having anyone telling us what to do. No one to decide we were too young to choose the scary rides or telling us not to dawdle and explore behind the sideshow tents where barkers described a calf with two heads, a bearded lady, or a woman with alligator skin. On the way to the Ferris wheel, I shouted, "Look at this!" as I pulled Carol under a canopy. "Steam shovels! Just look at all the good stuff you can win!"

There in the glass cubicles were miniature steam shovels surrounded by treasures too wonderful to resist. Figurines, rings, bracelets, and dolls beckoned to us. There were riches for our brothers as well. All one had to do was turn the crank and the machine would clamp its jaws on your favorite trinket. Reel it in and the prize was yours. What could be easier? And it only cost a dime! Anybody could see it was worth a lot more than ten cents. Confidently, we deposited our dimes and turned the crank.

"I'm getting the statue of the girl and the dog," I told Carol.

"I'm trying for the bracelet," she said.

We each grasped our prize in the shovel's mouth. Slowly, we turned the crank as it moved jerkily toward its goal. Suddenly the statuette slipped from my shovel's jaws. Again and again, I lost it before I could drop it into the tunnel. Before long, I needed to deposit another dime. Carol's shovel still clutched the bracelet. "I think you're going to make it," I whispered, just before it fell.

"Let's try it again. This time we'll surely get them," I urged. Over and over we tried, grasping objects only to drop them.

Finally, Carol said, "I have just enough money to take a ride on the Ferris wheel. Want to come with me?"

"You go ahead," I told her, "I'm going to try this one more time." When she came back, I was down to my last dime. This time, I focused on a pearl-handled jackknife for my brother Dennis, and then my last dime was gone.

The afternoon was long with no money to spend. Enviously, we watched the octopus ride whirl overhead. We yearned to be among the screaming passengers, scared and thrilled at the same time. Our parched throats longed for the cold velvet of ice-cream cones being slurped down by folks who hadn't wasted their money on steam shovels. Our tongues watered as theirs lapped the melting goodness to keep it from trickling down the side of the cone. Hot dog and popcorn aromas reminded us of our too early lunch.

When it was time to meet Daddy, we plopped onto the cool green grass under the shade of a tree. "Oh, oh, I just remembered what Mama said," Carol reminded me, "about not wasting our money on shills. What's she going to say when we tell her?"

"Well . . ." I reasoned, "It wasn't exactly a shill. It was a steam shovel." After a moment, I added quietly, "But let's not tell her anyway, okay?"

"Okay," she said. We sat thinking for a while.

"Know what?" I asked her.

"What?"

"I'm never going to try one of those things again!"

"Me neither!" Carol said.

When Daddy drove up, he kept the motor running while we hopped into the back seat. He rarely carried on a conversation with his children, and this time we were grateful for the silence as we rode the five miles home.

When we walked in, Mama was frying fresh side pork in the warm kitchen. The potatoes were boiling, and there was a johnnycake in the oven. Mama told Carol and me to run quickly to the garden and pick a few tomatoes for supper. Later, when we were shucking off our hot shoes and blue jeans, Mama asked, "Did you have a good time at the fair?"

"Yes," we said.

"What did you do?" she asked.

"Nothing," we answered.

BANG THE DRUM SOFTLY

By Tamara McClintock

Marriage, baby, divorce, death of a loved one—all huge branching-off points. But what about the seemingly inconsequential branching points? The ones that, upon further reflection, did have a contribution to an individual's life?

I remember a special field trip in fifth grade. Our class was bused to St. Paul to see the Minnesota Orchestra perform. I was mesmerized throughout the concert, and when our teacher gave us the opportunity to join the fifth- and sixth-grade elementary school band, I jumped at the chance. It just came down to the decision of what instrument to play. The horn section? I remember seeing trumpet players like Louis Armstrong on TV, and their lips looked kind of weird. If that's what horn playing did to the lips, I wasn't interested. I wanted my lips to look great, so some boy would want to kiss them in the future. Then there were the woodwinds. Too much slobbering. The flute? Flute players had to keep their arms in a warped pose like misshapen tree branches. Percussion? Well, one perk was the variety. There wasn't just one instrument in the percussion section; in addition to the snare drum, there were cymbals, triangle, tambourine, slide whistle, castanets, gong, bongos, and woodblock. Having played the piano, I could read musical notes, so I could also play the chimes, xylophone, bells, timpani, or marimba. I had made my decision and promptly signed up for band.

My parents took me to a music store and bought me drumsticks and one of those rubbery practice pads so I could practice drumming quietly at home. And then I saw it: a shiny, blue-spangled Ludwig snare drum! Just like Ralphie's obsession with the Red Ryder rifle in *A Christmas Story*, I became obsessed with getting this spectacular drum for Christmas. I dropped hints to my parents that were as subtle as sledgehammers. My anticipation grew as Christmas Eve got closer and closer. Finally, the night had come, and I opened my presents. No snare drum. My fervent wish was crushed.

On Christmas morning, when I got up to go to the bathroom, I spied something in the living room. There was the shiny, blue-spangled Ludwig snare drum all set up! I immediately had to try it out, even though everyone else was still sleeping. I didn't think they'd mind . . .

Our family moved twice during my junior high years. My sister found it tough adjusting to a new school each time, but I immediately joined the school band wherever I was. Band was the perfect place to find new friends; it was my security blanket.

High school band provided an outlet for my competitive nature. At the beginning of each year, band members had to audition for the band director, who would then rank us into chairs. For percussionists, the first chair got dibs on what percussion instrument they wanted to play for each piece. The way to move up was to challenge the chair above you to a match, and the band director would decide who won. I kept issuing challenges and kept moving on up, until I finally reached my goal. Of course, that meant a number of hours practicing at home. Looking back, I feel great sympathy for my family, having their peace disturbed by all the rat-a-tat-tatting. But when I came home from solo contests with top medals to show my proud parents, I hope it made up for the times when they might have regretted buying that Christmas present.

On occasion, participation in band taught me to anticipate potential problems. In the summer, band members wore heavy black blazers and pants as well as overlays for our uniforms when marching in parades. One year, we were marching in the Minneapolis Aquatennial in ninety-five-degree weather and one fourth of our drum section passed out from the heat. As each one started to pitch forward, designated personnel on the sides would run into the line, grab the drummers—who were still attached to their drums—and drag them to safety. Dodging the falling bodies, I kept drumming and marching like the Energizer bunny. Knowing the band would be marching in insufferable heat, I'd had the foresight to wear a bathing suit under my uniform.

Being in band was also a character builder. When I was zealously beating the timpani, one of the drums fell forward, crushing a few of the trombone players. I learned to say sorry when these kinds of situations arose. I also learned that it's sometimes best, when sitting with the band in the bleachers during a football game, to pretend it wasn't me who crashed the cymbals to punctuate a cheer for a touchdown, then found out it was the other team's touchdown. But I hadn't been paying attention, because I had been flirting with another drummer, who I was hoping would ask me to the dance.

The memories of the Christmas songs we played at the Christmas band concerts occasionally come flooding back. As a senior in high school, I played the temple blocks for "Sleigh Ride." The temple blocks simulated the sound of horse hooves. While playing this song at the concert, the rubber tip of one of the mallets popped off, and I was frantically trying to play with one mallet. It sounded as if the horse suddenly became lame in one leg, thus jeopardizing the sleigh occupants. One of the freshmen percussionists rushed across the stage after the rolling ball tip. The visual image of a panicked band member bolting through the group during the middle of a concert had me giggling through the rest of the number. I still find myself giggling when I hear "Sleigh Ride" playing in a store, much to the puzzlement of surrounding shoppers.

The decision to join band as a fifth grader was instrumental (sorry for the pun) in providing me with the opportunity to find friendships, appreciate music, and create fond memories. I will always be proud to have been a band geek!

BECOMING

By Cathy Peterson

As much as I enjoyed being a tomboy, climbing trees, hunting for craw-dads, going fishing, playing baseball, or hanging out with my two best buddies, who were both named David, I loved being a girl more. Going to church on Sunday mornings wearing a full-skirted dress with ruffled layers of a petticoat underneath was so awesome! As a girl, I was taught to be prim, proper, and good-mannered, keeping my hands folded and my legs together. Girls were meant to be seen, not heard. I was to behave in a "ladylike" way. I tried my best but not always with success! I was either too curious or running off to make mudpies, which does have a domestic flair to it.

Yet, as a girl, being impatient for my body to change was truly a wait-ing game. All of my friends got boobs, while I waited and waited. Would they ever arrive? Being a puny kid didn't help. Finally, when I was thirteen going on fourteen, the arrival had begun. I also had my first kiss then. Out behind the neighbor's garage in the alley, Kent, my first boyfriend, and I had decided to meet up to share a kiss. What a wonder it was in the cold December night—a cold kiss, but one never forgotten. To this day, I love a cold kiss. It was all so innocent and breathtaking as we watched our breath rise in the frosty, wintery air. We laughed joyously, and I knew the sensual feeling of being a blooming girl growing into womanhood.

But becoming a teenage young lady is complicated. The task at hand was to get an education, but, at the same time, find your Romeo! "Wherefore art thou, Romeo?" It seemed that the guys' hormones kicked in way before mine did! The pressure was also on to explore the realm of sex. I easily made it beyond high school before succumbing to any desire for intimacy. College contained more tension yet, as none of my friends were waiting for marriage. Back in the 1970s, finding a husband was an important aspect of a girl's life. It was called getting your MRS degree. Instead, I believed a girl should be like a butterfly—pretty to see but hard to catch. That also didn't work out all that well, because I was married by the time I was a fledgling of twenty-two, without much experience or any example of what a good marriage really looked like. Uh-oh! What had I done?

When marriage happens, the woman, the wife, is expected to know how to bake and cook. Our first Christmas being married, I was gifted with an authentic Betty Crocker cookbook. I tried not to be too offended, but it was all about his expectation and my obligation. A few red flags surfaced at this new stage of matrimony. This was a time to turn my frustration and edification to food.

And so, there's carbs! Snacks like chips, Cheetos, Fritos, and all the wonderful pastries, donuts, and breads—a woman *needs* them. Carbs, the most important part of a meal, of course, mean a baked potato, fries, or any kind of potato. Women have unending cravings for them. And then came an extra twenty pounds of snacks and carbs hanging on my frame.

Well then, let's add in the chocolate! Some would say having a balanced diet is having a piece of chocolate in both hands! Chocolate is the answer, so who cares what the question is? You can't buy happiness, but you can buy chocolate, and that's pretty much the same thing. Yes, it helps. Ask any woman! As a comparison, being a woman in the married world of baking is like "trying to be a beautiful cupcake in a world filled with muffins." I was, unfortunately, a muffin, the Pillsbury Doughboy kind!

How many times as a woman have I also stated, "I don't have anything to wear!" Of course, we have things to wear. You can see all your stuff in your closet from where you are exclaiming your distress, fully dressed. What any woman really means is, "I don't have anything to wear for whom I want to be today." My philosophy has come to this: "Life isn't perfect, but your outfit can be. Be less bitter, find more glitter, stay focused, and keep hunting for that perfect bargain and perfect fit." It is a woman's right. Here's a quick poem I wrote recently:

"Give me lots of jewelry and delicate lace, for I am a girly girl.
Make me a pretty and colorful dress, one in which to twirl.

May I live in a world filled with style and fashion,
Where I can truly live out my womanly passion.
Let me strive to be a sparkling lady all of my life.
Even though I have to be a hard-working wife."

And here are some quips and quotes that reflect being and becoming a woman I am passing on for posterity (most of which were found on the internet, of course).

<u>Words to live by</u>:

Be a Girl with a mind, a Woman with attitude, and a Lady with class. — Andrew Grewal

I am not what happened to me, I am what I choose to become. — Carl Gustav Jung

You're allowed to scream, you're allowed to cry, but never give up. — Brad Turnbull

Little girls with dreams become women with vision. — Achyuta Samanta

Women have been trained to speak softly and carry a lipstick. Those days are over. — Bella Abzug

Above all, be the heroine of your life, not the victim. — Nora Ephron

A strong woman loves, forgives, walks away, lets go, tries again, and perseveres . . . — Mandy Hale

A girl is much more than she seems, not a toy by any means; Underneath that makeup and hair, there's a sign that says, "Handle with care." — #455 The OneRule.com

It's hard to be a woman. You must think like a man, act like a lady, look like a young girl, and work like a horse. — Hilary Clinton

She is clothed in strength and dignity, and she laughs without the fear of the future. — Adapted from Proverbs 31:25

Here's to chasing your dreams in the cutest pair of shoes you own. — Clarita Gultiano

Cinderella never asked for a prince. She asked for a night off and a dress. (Then she got some pretty awesome shoes, too!) — Kiera Cass

A strong woman looks a challenge dead in the eye and gives it a wink. — Gina Carey

It's a fact that women live longer than men. But for my last act of trying to ever be a sexy woman, I want to be cremated in the hopes I will finally have a "smokin' hot body" (taken from Sybil Hick's obituary)! Now it's time to go change into some sweats!

Cinnamon Rolls

By Patsy Magelssen

Be prepared. You never know when you might meet Him . . .

December 6, 1990

It was a cold and blistery day in Owatonna, Minnesota, and I buttoned the top button on my coat and pulled my hat farther down on my head as I got out of the car. The street had been torn out for a water main problem, and mud was everywhere I needed to walk.

As I tiptoed through the slush and mud from the street under construction, I saw a yellow hard hat rising out of the manhole cover. The man had on a hooded jacket, and his eyes were twinkling in his weathered face. He had a full beard, and he was smiling as he exited the manhole, covered with mud from the heel of his boot to his waist. With an outstretched arm he shouted, "Wow, are those for me?"

"No way!" I replied, as I carefully carried the beautiful plate of frosted cinnamon rolls fresh from the oven. They were going to our garage mechanic across the street.

I'd had a plan that day: rise at 5:00 a.m., set two huge batches of sweet bread dough, let it rise, punch it down, let it rise again, bake and frost fourteen pans of cinnamon rolls. Each were now frosted and in baskets going to people I knew: widows, birthday persons, and people who had done favors for my nonprofit group during the year, like the radio station and newspaper. After all, I was on my way to Miller Automotive, who had recently fixed my flat tire. I had things to do and places still to go.

But there was something in his look, this man emerging from the manhole. It haunted me as I returned to the car. Had I just said no to

Jesus? Doesn't the Bible say, "When you do something, it is as if you did it for Jesus?"

I peeled the card and tape off the last batch of rolls, knowing I'd have a chance to make them for Pastor Vann another day. I skipped with joy as I carried the rolls back across the street and teasingly said, "You know, I *did* bake these just for you!" What a smile was on that muddy man's face!

I made a new note: "Pastor Vann, Merry Christmas! IOU a pan of cinnamon rolls." Then I dropped it off at church.

Nature Will Find a Way

By Tamara McClintock

Graduate from high school. Go to college. Find a husband. Have babies. Such was the path of the girls in my high school senior class. I graduated from high school. I went to college. I wasn't looking for, but accidentally found, a husband. Have babies? Uh, no. Naturally, my husband and I had discussed it, but we were never on the same page at the same time on this idea.

To me, children were synonymous with a lack of freedom. I was a type A personality, with lined up goals: get a master's degree in theater, get experience teaching high school, and get paid to act in and direct plays.

Eight years later, I had my MFA, had taught high school for five years, and was getting paid to act and direct at a dinner theater. My proverbial biological clock was ticking, but I didn't intend to replace the batteries.

Being on the pill had been insurance I wouldn't have to worry about getting pregnant, but having been on it for a prolonged period had resulted in some unpleasant side effects. My doctor suggested going off the pill and using the fertility awareness–based method, also known as the ovulation method or the natural family planning method.

"But we're not *planning* to have a family," I said.

"The ovulation method can be used to *prevent* as well as to *achieve* a pregnancy," was the response. So, I embarked on a meticulous method of charting my monthly cycles. Our passionate, spontaneous lovemaking morphed into a "Let's check the chart" ritual.

After a year and a half of this, I felt I had all the charting down to an exact science, but just as mathematician Dr. Malcolm, the chaos theorist, warned in *Jurassic Park*, "Nature will find a way." And it did. After taking a home pregnancy test affirming what I already had begun to suspect, I called my husband at work and told him, "Guess what? The rabbit died."

"What?" It took a bit for his brain to decode the meaning of that sentence, and he was shocked. But thankfully, the shock gave way to excitement.

If there ever was a good time for me to get pregnant, this was it. The theater production I was acting in was at the end of its run. Knowing that, physically, I was about to pop, I decided taking a temporary phone sales job would be the best way to bring in extra money. In my spare time, I spent hours reading La Leche literature and parenting books. If I was to enter this unknown territory, I wanted to be prepared.

The last few months of my pregnancy were hell. My doctor said I had toxemia, which was very dangerous. The mother or the baby, or both, could die. One of my aunts had had toxemia during one of her pregnancies, which resulted in a miscarriage. For eight years, I had gone to great lengths to avoid having children, but now I was desperate to keep this little baby alive. I meditated often to keep my skyrocketing blood pressure from going any higher, and my husband suggested I avoid watching television programs that were stressful, so *Cheers* instead of *Murder, She Wrote*.

At last, I went into labor, and my husband drove me to the hospital. I opted out of having drugs because I wanted my baby to come into the world fully alert and drug-free. My husband was the perfect coach, calming me down with his deep, radio voice. After eleven hours of grueling, painful labor, our little boy arrived. As exhausted and sore as I was, when the doctor put our new baby in my arms, I felt boundless joy. The name *Ian* means *God's gracious gift*, and I marveled that after a difficult and traumatic pregnancy, I was able to receive this inestimable treasure.

Because I hadn't had any drugs during labor, Ian emerged fully awake. Then came the moment. One transcendent moment where nothing else in the room existed. Just mother and baby gazing at each other in wonder.

THE SINGING RACER

By Elena Bookstrom White

Before I turned five, I chose to stay warm at Grandma Lisa's house in Denver and play with my cousin, Lorraine. We played jacks and "house" down by the lion's paws of Grandma's round oak table, the same table now in Minnesota, where I am writing this. Back then, my mom rued the fact that whenever they included me in the weekly family ski trip to the mountains, it would be a bitterly cold, windy day at Berthoud Pass. One day when I was persuaded to go to the ski area, we finally had better weather. But still I balked at learning to ski from my parents. On a snowy day, since the handsome ski instructor didn't have any other pupils, he offered to take me on. That's when I became a more enthusiastic part of my skiing family. I developed such a wide snowplow to ski down the part of a trail called "The Face" that I was the envy of the less flexible Ski Patrollers who had to prove they could snowplow down The Face in front of a rescue toboggan. It was said I could snowplow down an elevator shaft.

Back in the day, we had the distinction of being crazy folk for this odd leg-breaking passion for skiing. As the little one, I had my ups and downs. Riding the rope tow up the Practice Hill was easy for me because I just had to ride between the skis of my mom or dad with my arms wrapped back around their legs, while they did the work of hanging on to the heavy, twisting rope. The chairlift on the Big Hill was even more exciting, but as the chair rose over the lip of the steep part of the hill and into the blast of wind for the last half of the ride, my mom would shelter me as best she could while telling me over and over to wiggle my toes to keep them warm. Ha! (Much later, on a cold, windy chairlift ride with my son, he remembered cold ski days with my mom, his Grandma Lil, and how it was she who had taught him to be tough.)

My older brother, Art, had more fun on the chairlift because he and his friend Billy pretended to be World War II bombardiers, laying waste to the slopes below. That play waned when he started entering junior ski races. I soon caught that bug, too, when I got a third-place medal (out of three) in my first race and met a skiing friend my age. This racing fever led to travel farther afield. After a downhill race at Steamboat Springs, a gatekeeper who had watched and heard me ski by remarked to me and my parents that I was the only racer who was so relaxed as to be singing! I felt embarrassed by this laughable revelation and never sang in a race again.

There were other turning points in my ski-racing career that kept me at it. In ninth grade, I had the happy surprise of earning a place on the Southern Rocky Mountain Team for the Junior Nationals in Franconia, New Hampshire. When we arrived, the ski lifts were not running because the ice was deemed too dangerous for skiing after the heavy rain from the day before had frozen solid. We Westerners were in shock when we found we could barely climb up that black ice to practice slalom. The next surprise was on the first race day, when after what felt like a dreadful run, skidding wide around the slalom poles, I got fourth place over many more-seasoned racers. That day, many girls were tearful and many boys were angry about the way they had skied.

One of the best ski runs of my life was four years later, the day I failed to make the Junior National Team after having been on it for three years and had been seeded first in slalom in the region. It was my last year as a junior racer, my last chance! But in the final qualifying slalom, I caught a tip and spun out. My world and self-image were crushed. After hiding with my tears of despair for a while, I rode up the T-bars to the top of Winter Park and skied the moguls on Bradley's Bash like a madwoman. Yes, I was *mad*! And I don't think I had ever skied better. I was quick, supple, and rhythmic. It was then that I understood why some family friends used to try to say things to make me angry when I was at the starting gate.

After many college races and ski stories later, the end of my identity as a ski racer came when my husband got a job in mountainless St. Cloud, Minnesota. For our survival, he taught me how to cross-country ski. But when I go out West to alpine ski with my brother, I have rediscovered I don't have to get mad to ski well, nor do I need to be upset over a bad run. I'm skiing just for fun, and I ski best when I sing out loud, to the amusement of the folks overhead on the chairlift.

THE COSTUME KEEPER

By Elena Bookstrom White

Lisa Anderson, my mom's mom, was a dynamo in keeping Swedish tradi-
tions alive. She prepared the Christmas smorgasbord for weeks, from soaking
the cardboard-like flank of a dried fish that would reconstitute into lutefisk,
to pickling a brisket in a crock, to hand-stuffing her liver körv and flask
körv (pork sausage with ginger—no potatoes!) among other dishes. When
visitors came to her house, she used to point to the worn-out ring in the car-
pet around her oak table with pride, evidence of how much she and her two
daughters had danced hambo, polka, and schottische around the table to the
music on the old wind-up Victrola record player. She attended two Swedish
Lodges (fraternal organizations) that put on Christmas and Midsummer
celebrations and provided her with a community of Swedish speakers.

She came to the United States and to Denver, Colorado, in 1905, and
returned to Sweden for a visit in 1912. (The story goes that she had a ticket
for the Titanic, but since it didn't make it to the US, she went over on a
different ship.) At that time, there was a revival of interest in folk tradi-
tions, including provincial clothing and dances. She brought fabrics back
home to make costumes representing her home province, Östergötland,
and the Dalarna costume, which, at that time, represented Sweden before
a national costume was designed. At Swedish celebrations, folks would ask
each other what province their costume was from.

Otto Bookstrom, my dad's father, immigrated to Boston but later
came to Denver to recover from tuberculosis. He worked as a train me-
chanic. As a member of the Swedish community in Denver, he was the
director of the Swedish language plays. Grandma Lisa acted in those plays.

One year, the Swedish theater group did a play, *Värmläningar*, that
featured some folk dances. They recruited the young people of the Swedish

community to dance, in costume, of course. At the time, my dad, Hans, was in high school and my mom, Lil, was in junior high. Daddy had a roadster he named Scrambola that had a rumble seat in the back. Mom, just the kid of the group, was relegated to the outside rumble seat on rides to and from rehearsals.

A few years later, the same play was repeated. Now in high school, Mom was promoted to the front seat with my dad. During the Depression, when Daddy was excited to be hired by a print shop, they decided they could afford to get married. They went on a brief honeymoon, only to find out when they drove by the print shop upon their return that it had burned to the ground. So, Daddy's role was to drive Mom to her work at Montgomery Ward in the wee hours of the morning. Since he would be in his pajamas, he always worried he would get a flat tire.

Sometime before World War II, they formed a performing group, the Hans Bookstrom Swedish Folk Dancers of Denver. The family costumes were back in play. Daddy now worried he would get a flat tire when he was driving to a performance in his yellow knickers, red stockings, and flowered vest. In addition to the dances that had been performed in the play, Mom and Grandma Lisa translated the directions and reconstructed several regional figure dances from various provinces. When my brother, Art, and I came along (1938 and 1941, respectively), Grandma and Mom made costumes for us, and when we were old enough, we performed a kids' dance. I remember performing for Swedish celebrations and at the Lowry hospital for injured soldiers sometime after the war.

As time went on, it became more and more difficult to get the group together for rehearsals and performances. Eventually, it would often be just our family and our accordion player performing for holidays, church groups, and international festivals. Altering the costumes to fit my brother and me was an ongoing process as we grew. One time, we danced in a junior high talent show. That's when Art decided to concentrate on playing accordion rather than dance in front of his peers.

In retirement, he has found much more time for playing accordion, and I continue to dance. The family costumes are tucked away in my closet, and I feel a responsibility to preserve them, though Mom's summer Östergötland apron has a worn hole where her sweaty free hand was on her hip, and the formerly red stripes on a Dalarna apron are faded to orange.

Long ago, my grandma had loaned it to a friend who spilled something on it and then had it professionally dry-cleaned against Grandma's express stipulations. Only Grandma Lisa knew how to dry-clean it properly. (For many years, Grandma had done dry-cleaning as well as laundry, ironing, and housecleaning for wealthy Denver families.) The costumes, seldom cleaned, ironed, or worn anymore, hold family and cultural tradition, quietly in the dark. My closet may be their final museum.

TALKING STICK

By Jerry Wellik

sitting in a circle
passing the "talking stick"
Being with friends.

Listening intent ears
no other cares
my favorite activity

in this world
listening to stories
a circle of friends

ROMANCE ON THE ROOF

By Tamara McClintock

It's supposedly the job of parents to give their kids the "sex talk" at some point. But, since most parents find it awkward or embarrassing, Ann Landers decided she could be the one parents and teens could turn to for guidance on this delicate subject.

In the late sixties, Landers composed a sexual questionnaire for teenagers, which was published in newspapers across the country. There were a series of questions like "Do you drink?" "Have you ever gotten or given a hickey?" "Have you ever gone all the way?" Each question was worth a certain number of points, and when you tallied up your points, you matched the score with the corresponding categories. These categories were in order of moral integrity and read as follows:

Pure as the Driven Snow
Passionate but Prudish
Normal and Decent
Indecent
Headed for Serious Trouble
In Terrible Shape
Condemned

At the end of eighth grade, I was still "Pure as the Driven Snow." My eighth grade focus was on confirmation class—until the summer, when my family moved to the southeast part of town. Just one block away lived this cute guy who was in the school band with me. He had dark, curly hair and Paul Newman–blue eyes.

One evening after supper, Peter invited me over to his house. When I got there, we sat on the sofa talking. Then, he slid closer and kissed me, which I really liked, followed by a French kiss, which I thought was pretty slimy. Now, plain kissing and French kissing added more points to my Ann Landers questionnaire, and it occurred to me that I was no longer "Pure as the Driven Snow"—now, I was "Passionate but Prudish." I was fine with that. It also dawned on me that his parents must not be home. I wondered if they would approve of him being alone with a girl. I knew my parents wouldn't.

I started to think I should leave when, suddenly, a car drove up in the driveway and Peter jumped up off the couch in a panic and yelled, "Oh, no! It's my mom! You have to get out of here!" I had never been in his house before and didn't know where the back door was. By that time, his mother was opening the front door, so I flung open the door nearest to me, which unfortunately led upstairs. I had nowhere to go but up.

The upstairs was an attic with two small rooms—Peter's bedroom and a den. I was worried his mother would come upstairs, so I tried to find a hiding place. I went into Peter's room and attempted to squish my body under his bed, but even thin as I was, the bed was just too close to the floor. I crept as silently as possible into the den and looked around. There didn't seem to be a good hiding spot there either.

Peter came upstairs and whispered, "Crap! Now my mom says I need to take a bath!" He grabbed his pajamas and went downstairs. He was fifteen years old, and his mom was still telling him when to take a bath?! A few minutes later, I heard footsteps on the stairs. I knew it was his mom because Peter would be in the bathtub by now. No doubt she had heard a noise upstairs and was coming to investigate. I was in the den at the time, and I dove under the desk.

The footsteps first entered Peter's bedroom, and I heard the closet door open and shut. Then I heard the footsteps walking out, and I saw her feet standing in the doorway of the den. I knew that if she came all the way into the room, then turned to go out, she would have a direct view of me. What in the world would I say? I tried to think of scenarios that would explain why I was crouching under the desk, but my mind was a total blank. I held my breath. The feet in the doorway turned and went back downstairs. I was saved—at least for the moment.

I crept slowly back into Peter's room and saw the window in his room was open and there was direct access to the roof. Gingerly, I climbed out the window. I was wearing shorts, and the rough, muddy, wet shingles scraped my legs. There I sat, looking down at the patio below. Maybe I'd get lucky and not be injured if I jumped off the roof. Maybe jumping off the roof might be a plan to get me out of this mess. (Sidebar: the rational part of a teen's brain isn't fully developed, so I had an excuse for my irrational feeling that jumping off a roof was a better option than going downstairs and facing Peter's mother.)

Peter came back upstairs in his pajamas, and despite my plight, I remembered that one of the questions in the Ann Landers questionnaire was, "Have you ever seen a member of the opposite sex in his or her pajamas?" I thought that was a pretty dumb question—especially since his pajamas looked like something an eight-year-old would wear. Still, because I had seen him in his pajamas, I would now have to answer yes to that quiz question, which added more points to my score, bumping me down to the next category of "Normal and Decent." I could accept that. Normal and Decent was okay. I was normal and decent; that wasn't bad.

When Peter saw me sitting on the roof, he was alarmed and leaned out the window. "I think I'm going to try to jump," I said.

"No! I can't let you do that!" were his compassionate words. As he grabbed me to try to pull me back in, his hand brushed against my breast. Shoot! Was that first or second base? Whichever one it was, my breast had just been touched, which propelled me to the "Indecent" category!

Suddenly, we both heard his mother's footsteps on the stairs. He quickly released me, and his caring words, "I can't let you do that," became, "If you're gonna jump, you better do it now." I slid my rear end to the edge of the roof—and jumped! My body dropped like a lead weight and my sandaled feet smacked the bricked patio below. Amazingly, I was still standing, but my body was vibrating from the shock wave that went from my feet all the way up to my head, reminiscent of Wile E. Coyote in the Road Runner cartoons. I did a quick check to see if all my parts still worked, then dashed down the alley while reflecting that, in the space of one hour at Peter's house, I had blown through three of Ann Landers's survey categories, and I still had three whole years of high school left!

Years later, I was mingling at my high school reunion when I came face-to-face with a man who had dark, curly hair and Paul Newman–blue eyes. The first words out of his mouth were, "Do you remember when you jumped off my roof?"

Remember? How could I ever forget?

STAGECRAFT

By Jim Romanowsky

All the world is a stage
And our lives
One act plays
Running in real time
Right now
With no repeat
Performances

Let's hope
We've learned
Our lines well
They are what
People will
Remember about us

HALLOWEEN MEMORIES IN THE 1940S

By Patsy Magelssen

We lived on a little dairy farm in Wisconsin during the Depression. It was about one and a half miles off the county blacktop road and down at the end of a gravel road. Times were tough, but I cannot remember going to bed hungry. Father always brought home some kind of meat from the woods, and mother always got out the canned jars of vegetables from the root cellar. The little grocery store in town gave Mother credit until we could pay for staples like sugar and flour. You just got by with what you had. The whole country was in need.

During the summer, we spent a lot of time growing things to eat in Mother's huge vegetable garden. She would can them in Ball quart jars, using the big presser cooker that processed eight jars' worth at a time. One year, after much begging followed by much coaching, Mom let me have a special place in her garden to grow pumpkins. After all, she could cook them up for pumpkin pie, I reasoned with her.

It was just not her favorite plant. You make a little hill of soil and plant four seeds at top of the mound—only four. You then leave about three feet of soil on all sides for the plant to branch out. I had all the instructions from Daddy. This year I would do it! I would have a pumpkin for the school program! I would *not* have to be a pilgrim with a stupid paper hat on my head in our one-room schoolhouse. Maybe I could even have a speaking part. I felt so brave.

When I was supposed to be weeding the carrots or picking the peas, I wandered over to my little mound to see if anything was happening. Finally, four little green leaves popped up. Week after week, I carefully watered the mound and put some cow-you-know-what on it (sounds horrible, but that's what Daddy said made things grow). I watched the vine tentacles branch out all over the place. This did not please Mother, and she cut off the ends because they were growing into the beet rows.

Big, orange, bell-shaped flowers grew into little balls, which grew larger each day. Daddy became interested in my pumpkin patch, and one day did something that about shook my heart apart and brought me to tears. He walked over to my precious plants and *cut off six of my little green balls*! Oh my, I thought I was going to die! How could he *do* that? "We want all the growth to be with *these* three pumpkins," he explained.

It did not make sense to me, but wow, did those three pumpkins grow. We watered and put the cow-you-know-what on the plants each day. I even let Mother cut off the vine ends, which were now heading for the beans, without crying out loud. I just held my heart and shook.

Come Halloween time, Daddy loaded those three *huge* pumpkins into the tractor metal box and drove me to school. Down that one-and-a-half-mile gravel road we rolled. I stood in the metal box and waved at Lucille and Gary Brown as we passed them walking to school. They had their mouths wide open in surprise as they carried their dinky little pumpkins that day. Daddy had made wooden stands to hold the pumpkins because they were too big for me to hold.

There I stood that afternoon in October 1949, in third grade and in the center of the Halloween program with my pumpkins on each side. I recited a poem I had written. Daddy had to go back to milk the cows, but Mother and baby Richard were in the audience. It was a very proud moment.

As farmers, we didn't cut the top off the pumpkins, gut them, and cut out scary faces to make jack-o'-lanterns. We cooked them and made pumpkin pies. It wasn't until I moved to Minneapolis in sixth grade that I even heard of trick-or-treating and cutting faces in the pumpkins. They let the pumpkins sit on their front steps until they rotted.

So, when I was in the sixth grade at my new school, Loring Elementary, kids started knocking on our front door in crazy costumes. They demanded treats, and Mother gave them a cookie, an apple, or some candy we just happened to have in the house. I figured this was a pretty good deal. I got a bag, went next door, and yelled, "Trick or treat!"

That first lady asked, "Where is your costume?"

The lady at the next house said, "Aren't you too old to be doing this?"

That was the extent of my Halloween filling-a-bag-with-candy—a piece of chocolate and a sucker. Not much to talk about.

My Tour of Duty in Panama

By James Ellickson

General Torrijos went to a bull fight in Mexico City in the fall of 1969. There was a coup, and a group of Panamanian generals took over the government in Panama City. Instead of flying back to Panama, Torrijos flew to an airport in Costa Rica and started to march south along the Pan-American Highway. The people marched with him to Panama City and encircled the National Guard headquarters. The US forces issued weapons to our MPs, and everyone settled in to watch the show. The Torrijos government said in the press that no one was hurt in this "internal" event, but our guys saw them dragging dead bodies off the roof.

So that was Panama when I arrived in January 1970. I worked in a computer room in a tunnel deep in a mountain overlooking the Panama Canal. I had a high clearance for key-punching information into a classified database. That's all I can tell you because that's all I knew.

No, there was one more thing. We received a new computer while I was there. An IBM 360! It was shipped through the canal to the dock on the Pacific side, then loaded on a truck, and gingerly transported to the cave. Our captain was overjoyed. We could replace the punch cards.

But there was yet one more surprise going on that I didn't understand at the time. The United States had a ninety-nine-year lease for the canal, and the lease was coming to an end. So, the decision was made (at the highest levels) to begin the transition to Panamanian control of the canal operation. The US military presence was reduced and moved to Florida. My punch cards became payroll records for the soldiers, and I was moved to another Army base north of the canal. Things were changing, but not fast enough for the Panamanians. There was friction between the people living and working in the Zone, (who considered themselves US citizens), and those people living in the Republic of Panama proper. After getting it all set up, Captain Richardson had to see his brand-new computer packed up and shipped back to Florida.

My wife, Ellen, became pregnant that year, and she was medically discharged from the Navy. She could spend her second trimester with me in Panama. I found an apartment in the city, and we rented a VW Bug from a sergeant I worked with. Driving to work in the Bug, I learned the Panamanian custom of always waiting for three cars to go through a light that had turned from yellow to red, honking all the way, before it was safe to proceed across an intersection. Since I didn't speak Spanish, an accident would have been a very bad situation.

The travel agency below our apartment had a rotating sign that flashed in our window all night. And there were always cockroaches scattered across the floor in the night. We learned to turn on the light and watch them scatter before we could walk to the bathroom. We had three idyllic months living together as Ellen grew our first and only baby.

The story I wanted to tell you is a Christmas story. We were used to receiving an allotment check each month from the Army for Ellen, as she was my wife. But the December check was forwarded by ordinary first-class mail in the States (what we called, "boat mail") to my mailbox in Panama, and it had not yet arrived.

It was Christmas Eve, and we were completely out of food. We were Minnesota people, used to snow on Christmas, but there was no snow in sight in Panama. We felt very much alone, and we were very broke. Ellen was growing a baby, and we were both worried. Our plan was to go to a US military chapel for Christmas Eve worship services, but we stopped at the post office to look for the allotment check. There was no check. On our way back to our apartment after the service, we stopped by the post office again, for no real reason, just to check on the check.

There it was! We couldn't believe it. A Christmas present we really needed. We bought sodas and chips at a convenience store with the loose change in our pockets. We felt blessed for many reasons.

The other side of the story is that twenty-three years later, we returned to Panama to visit our daughter and her husband at their Peace Corps site in the hills north of Panama City. Our daughter accompanied us using Panamanian public transportation to a road leading up into the hills. We transferred to a pickup truck filled with local folks, and up into the hills we went. They hosted us in their little rental house without windows, and we went around to meet all their neighbors. We were "big stuff," people who were so rich and could travel all the way from the US to see Panama. We had a wonderful two weeks. Panama had successfully taken over canal operations by then.

Returning to 1970, Ellen had to fly back to the US to get ready for our civilian life. I flew back to the States to be discharged. I got as far as the Atlanta airport when I ran out of daylight. I couldn't get a military standby seat until the next day. So, I slept on a bench at the airport, in my uniform and next to my duffle bag. The next day, I caught my flight to Minneapolis-Saint Paul and met Ellen and her whole family. They brought me a warm jacket and snowshoes. It was great to be home again.

Courageous Mother

By Roseanna Gaye Ross

Lucille Commadore Bridges died today,
    and I cried.

She, the child of Mississippi sharecroppers,
    a stranger to me,
Lucille,
    housekeeper with an 8th grade education,
a hidden figure
    determined to create a better life for her baby,
making history.

At her side, 6-year-old daughter, Ruby,
    federal marshals,
        the US Supreme Court,
            "The United States President said we can,"
Proudly walking ebony-skinned Ruby to her all-white school,
    amid chants of protest,
        hurled eggs and tomatoes.

Did Lucille cry secret tears in her bed at night?
Were there silent questionings of doubt?
Did her steps reveal the bellyache of fear
    as she held Ruby's tiny hand?

Lucille Commadore Bridges died today,
    and I cried.
Moved by her courage.

Reminded of the courage of all the hidden figures,
Mothers who dream of something more,
    Aspirations with far less public drama, mothers who
Walk beside their babies daily,
Determined.

THE WEAVER

By Steven M. Hoover, PhD

I sit, observing as the nurse explains the process. She will say three words and ask my mother to repeat them back to her. She does, and Mom repeats them correctly. Next, the nurse asks her to draw a clock face with numbers and hands to represent ten minutes before 11:00. Mom executes this correctly, along with the date and the current president of the United States. Finally, she asks her for the three words again. Mom pauses, glances at me, and shrugs. They are gone. Later, haunted by this, I write:

Three simple words,
No threads with which to bind them.
Darkness weaves the loom.

TOE STORY 3

By Brad Busse

May 19, 1975. "A day that will live in infamy!"

It was a Friday. I'm sure of that. I had just finished my first year of college down in Memphis. I took my last exam Thursday afternoon, packed up everything from my dorm room, crammed it all into the back of my Pinto, and headed to Nashville.

Bad year. Goofy roommate. Unsatisfying classes. My girlfriend and I had been fighting a lot. I don't really remember why. She was the reason I had gone to Memphis State, and it just wasn't a good fit.

So, as I drove up I-40, I had time to think. I really didn't know what I wanted to do. I loved music, but I knew I wasn't good enough to make a living at it. My voice teacher and mentor said I had a nice voice, but I knew I was one of those people who was perfect for singing in a group. Definitely not a soloist, that's for sure.

One idea I had been toying with was joining the service. They'd ended the draft literally months before my eighteenth birthday. Although Vietnam had soured many young men on the idea, I felt very patriotic, and I knew that a stint in the service would allow me to save up money for college later. I made a mental note to call a Marine Corps recruiter when I got home.

When I pulled in, the house was empty. Both Mom and Dad were at work, and my little sister Amy wasn't home from school yet. My older sister Jill was attending Augsburg up in Minneapolis, and she had secured an internship somewhere, so she wouldn't be home much at all that summer.

My home was nice. Comforting. I had my own room, and Dad had helped me hang a wicker chair from the ceiling in a nook in the corner.

Instead of closet doors, we had hung beads! Just add in that shag carpeting, and my room was a classic seventies haven.

Amy came home from school. Mom came home, gave me a hug, and then made dinner, and when Dad got home, we had a nice meal. I casually mentioned my idea of joining the service. I saw Mom shoot Dad a look. They didn't say anything, but I knew they were worried. Dad, Army. Mom's two brothers, Navy and Coast Guard. Dad went to East Germany. He said half of the servicemen were like him, the other half went to Korea. He said many of them never came home.

I woke up Friday morning and had a cup of coffee while the folks dressed for work. Amy took off for school, and I had the house to myself.

Nice day, warm, but not too warm. Summers in Tennessee could be brutally hot, but since it was just May, the heat hadn't really started. I noticed the grass needed mowing. Now that was something I could do to contribute. I suddenly remembered about calling the recruiter, so I called and got a very nice voice on the other end. I told him about my interest, and he made an appointment for me the following Monday afternoon.

I pulled on some shorts and a T-shirt, found my old dumpy sneakers, and headed out. The mower was in the garage. I checked the oil, flipped it over and scraped out the dead grass, filled the tank, and started off. I decided to do the front yard first. Our yard was a good-sized one, mostly flat, but sloping down a little before it reached the road.

What happened next, I only remembered fully later. Years later.

I slipped. The grass was a little wet from the dew, but not too wet to mow. I fell backward and heard a loud BANG! Strangely, it didn't really hurt. Not like you would think it would. I looked down, and the front half of my right tennis shoe was gone. There was so much blood I couldn't tell exactly what I'd lost. The panic I felt was intense. I hobbled to the front door, then changed my mind and limped around to the back door. I didn't want to get blood on the carpet, and the kitchen had tile. Mom's never let me forget that blood on the carpet would not have been her top priority.

I grabbed the phone and dialed Mom's number at work. (There was no 911 back then, and I didn't know what to do.) Mom answered, and I said something like "I'm hurt." I'll never forget what she said.

"Who is this?"

"Mom, it's me. I fell under the lawn mower." She told me sit tight. I hung up and grabbed some paper towels to mop up the pool of blood on the floor. I took a closer look at my foot and realized I had lost my big toe. All the rest of my toes were untouched.

I heard a voice at the door. Mom had called a retired neighbor, good old Mr. Zumbro, and he came right over. He helped me bandage up my foot and then helped me to his car. I told him I didn't want to get blood all over his car, so he grabbed some towels and covered the floor on the passenger side. I guess I had the presence of mind to suggest he drive me to Dr. Renfro's clinic. I had worked as a janitor for him after school for several years, and his practice largely treated injuries like mine.

Mom went to the house to find my toe, wrapped it up, and brought it to the clinic. Dr. Renfro took one look at it and said it was too beat-up to save. So, he put a couple of stitches in and bandaged me up. Then he grabbed a pair of crutches and sent me on my way. Remember, this was in the dark ages. Today, they'd probably sew it back on.

I remember when Mom and I got home, everyone was so upset. Dad was out of town on business, so we had to relive the entire thing when he got home the next day. There wasn't much anyone could do. It honestly didn't hurt, but after a while, a steady ache settled in. Aspirin and elevation. It was about all I could do. The recruiter called Monday to ask why I hadn't shown up. It was all I could do not to sob when I told him what happened.

There were some tough times. Most people understand the concept of ghost pains. And I had those for more than a year afterward. But I also had ghost *itching*! It was unbelievably maddening not to be able to scratch that itch. I also couldn't wear flip flops. To this day, I only buy huarache sandals, the kind that covered the entire foot.

There isn't that much more to this story. The foot healed. I did some physical therapy to help me with my gait and balance. I remember the physical therapist was really cute. Mid-twenties. Dark hair. A real knockout.

"I didn't expect you to just *walk* in here," she said. Mustering up as much machismo as I could, especially because she was so good-looking, I played the whole thing down. She asked what I liked to do for exercise, and I told her I loved tennis. She did, too. So, for the next couple of appointments, we met at a tennis court, and I gingerly hobbled around and did my best.

Now, if this story was worth its salt, I would have wooed and won over the lovely therapist, married her, and lived happily ever after. Nope. I never saw her again. Sigh.

Since then, I have found ways to make fun of the whole thing. Humor is the armor I usually reach for first. I used to go shoe shopping and let the salesperson try on smaller and smaller shoes since he or she couldn't feel the big toe and thought the shoe was too big. (Go ahead. Groan.)

Once, a friend told me, "You'll never be a spy!" Why not? "You can't tip toe."

I also enjoyed telling whoever was nearby that my career as a football kicker was shot all to hell.

I got married. She (now my ex-wife) was a nurse, so nothing fazed her. And when we got our first house, we had a small television set on the dresser at the foot of the bed. I noticed that because of that missing toe, I could see the TV beautifully without having to move my legs. Both of my kids, when they were just toddlers, would stare at my foot in wonder. They'd look at my foot, then down at theirs, trying to grasp the difference. It's the small things, I guess.

I have now lived much longer without the toe than with it, and it's just a part of who I am. For years, I didn't tell anyone about it. I'm not sure why I've changed my mind, but now I don't seem to care as much. Part of being an old fart, I suppose.

So, needless to say, my life went in a different direction. I've often said, "God, if you didn't want me to go into the service, I would have taken a heart murmur." Now, ironically, I have one. God – 1. Me – 0.

I've related this saga many times verbally, but this is the first time I've written it down. The best part of relating this tale? The fact that I get to call it "Toe Story 3."

My Discovery of What Gender Identity Means to Me

By Lolly Loomis

When I was young, I loved being a girl. Boys were so ordinary, after all. They could only wear pants and shirts. They could never look "pretty" like girls could. Even when I wore pants and shirts, I could look "pretty." The colors were bright, and the shirts and pants could be of different styles. Boys always wore blue or black pants and ordinary shirts. And I loved wearing dresses—especially the kind with full skirts I could twirl. I could wear my hair long or short. I loved getting my Toni Home Permanents so I could have curly hair.

There were seven children in our family—four girls and three boys. We all had traditional boy/girl roles. I always thought the boys had it made because their work was always outside. We girls had to work in the house. I loved being outside, summer or winter, it didn't matter.

Then it happened—baseball. Definitely a guy thing, but I loved it. I loved watching it, but mostly I loved, loved playing it. But girls did *not* play baseball at that time. There was a group of boys from my neighborhood who played baseball in the field behind my house almost every day. Many times, I would sit on the side of the baseball diamond and watch while the boys played. One day, as they were choosing sides, they discovered they were one person short of having even teams. They started to argue about who was not going to play. The other choice was to go home and not play that day. That's when I spoke up and said I would be willing to play. They decided they had to let me play or not play at all that day. Then they had a fight about who would have to take "the girl." No one wanted me, of course. Finally, my brother, who was captain of one team, said he'd take me.

My debut! And the first time I remember breaking with traditional boy/girl roles. Everyone knew I was not a good runner, so they started me at first base to check my throwing arm. Turns out, I was a passable thrower and catcher. Now we were up to bat. Because of my lack of running ability, they figured that even if I hit the ball, I would be an "easy out." They were surprised when I went to bat knowing how to hold it correctly. I took the appropriate hitter's stance, as well. On the first two pitches, I swung and missed. I may have had a few balls in there, too, but it looked like I was indeed going to be the "easy out." On the next pitch, I took a swing. I connected! I hit it over the fence—it was a home run! Out of the four times I was at bat that day, I hit three home runs. It seems that if you hit home runs, you don't have to be a good runner. From then on, the boys wanted me to play baseball with them. They argued over which team would get me, because now *both* teams wanted me. I was so happy I would be able to play the game I loved.

I learned a lesson from this experience, but it never had a real effect on my life until much, much later. This is the lesson I learned: I could be pretty, be sweet, clean inside the house, play with dolls, and babysit, *and* I could compete with anyone. Girls could do some of the same things boys could do—and sometimes they could do them even better! But how this experience affected my life is another story.

GER

By Barb Flynn McColgan

Can you hear her voice—
        with its upbeat lilt saying,
        "Here, let me help you get this done!"

Can you hear her voice—
        soft and soothing as it cradles your worries
        in its loving touch?

Can you hear her voice—
        as she raises up prayers for you
        and for those you love?

Can you hear her voice—
        silent as she patiently listens
        to what you need to say?

Can you hear her voice—
        filled with compassion
        as she sees through your protective armor into your heart?

Can you hear her voice—
        letting you know
        it's okay, we all make mistakes.

Can you hear her voice—
>
> its musical tones filling you with happiness,
> rising up and floating light as a feather on a breeze?

Listen closely. Listen hard. Hear her voice on the wind, coming down from the heavens to say you are loved!

— Written for my beloved sister-in-law on the occasion of her untimely death.

MONEY

By Barb Flynn McColgan

We clamored in excited anticipation onto the school bus like a herd of buffalo fighting to get to a water hole.

"Slow down!"

"Take your time!"

"Be careful!" came the commands from our chaperones.

We were sixth graders, eleven and twelve years old, going to the circus—the Shrine Circus, sixty miles and an hour drive away! When you got to sixth grade, you got to do all sorts of cool things! You got to go on field trips, and you got to work on the coveted Minnesota scrapbook on Friday afternoons. You could volunteer to read to the kindergarteners (one of whom was my little sister), *and* you got to go to the Shrine Circus! Both of my older brothers had been able to taste the tantalizing world of the circus, and now, *finally*, it was my turn.

It was in the spring of 1965. We were going to the "big city" (population of 18,000 compared to our village of 550). What a great adventure! I don't remember who I sat with on the bus ride, though it might have been the other Barb, or Bobbie Jo, or Doris, who liked to be called Dodo. What I do remember is that I had *ten dollars*! Big money! I had $5 of my own, and my parents had given me $5. What would I spend it on? We ate our packed lunches on the ride up, so it didn't have to go for food. It was all mine to spend on snacks or souvenirs! What kind of goodies had my brothers brought home from their circus adventures? This was like having "mad money." It didn't *have* to be spent on anything specific, practical, or necessary. I could spend it on whatever I wanted! The possibilities I imagined were endless, as if I gazed into a bottomless treasure chest.

Upon reaching that big arena, we piled off our bus, finding it impossible to remain orderly as the adults had requested. We had been seated for a short time in our assigned section when the lights went up and the music started. My first ever circus!

I know there were probably elephants, clowns, aerialists, and trick horseback riders. I think there must have been tigers, lions, monkeys, and much more, but I don't really remember many specifics about the show. What I remember is wondering, pondering, fretting over what to buy with my "no-strings-attached" money. I went out into the lobby and checked out all the booths and kiosks with all the toys and souvenirs. Should I get a Shriners hat? A fancy balloon? Should I get one main thing or a bunch of smaller things? I had never had money to spend frivolously. This was a new experience for me. I was accustomed to considering what was the most reasonable and the most practical when I shopped. What would last the longest? What would I not tire of as quickly? Those rules simply did not apply here. It was like trying to apply Miss Manners rules of etiquette to a room full of loose monkeys: simply impossible!

When I returned to my seat inside the arena, I saw other kids come back with cotton candy, stuffed monkeys, brightly colored circus posters, and glasses with Shrine Circus splashed on the side in bold letters. With each new item I saw in the possession of one of my classmates, I thought, "Maybe that," or "Ooh, maybe I should get one of those!" or "That is so nifty, I wonder if I should . . .?" Each time, I pondered whether the item was worth spending my precious money on. I didn't want to spend it too soon, in case I later found something better!

Out I would go to the lobby area for another look. How about a clown nose and hat? Where would I wear them? A light-up spinner? Not "circusy" enough. A circus poster? Where would I hang it? Cotton candy went too fast. I think I maybe did buy a small bag of popcorn, but I don't remember for sure. Briefly in to watch the performers and then back out to the lobby I went, again and again, to look for the perfect souvenir. Over and over, I returned to my seat empty-handed.

And that is how my day at the circus went. I don't remember much about what the acts were, who I sat with, or what impressed me the most. I remember feeling torn and conflicted about what to buy with this very special "free-to-spend" money. Before I knew it, the time came to leave.

No, I was told, there was not time to stop at one of the stands to buy something. The adults in charge were sure there had been plenty of time to buy things all afternoon.

So, we got on the bus, and for the hour ride home, everyone showed off and played with their mementos, their souvenirs, their treasures from the circus. It was a quiet ride for me. I felt very sad, and I was very mad at myself for not buying *anything*!

There are many things we learn in life, not from direct instruction but from observation and inference. No one may ever have said, "Money is too hard to come by, so don't spend it foolishly," but you may have read that message in decisions your parents made, or you may have seen it in the expressions on their faces. Your mother and father may have avoided saying, "We can't afford that," but you saw how they never bought things for themselves, or that things never got thrown out but instead were always fixed or used again in one way or another.

And as we became adults, with our own money and our own bills, we formed our own thoughts and beliefs and rules about money. We developed our own approach to what role money should or shouldn't play in our lives. And though it may not always be obvious, if we look a little deeper, we will see woven in those ideas we absorbed from our parents and family, down below the surface, directly or indirectly, contributing to who we are today.

Addendum

I'm not completely sure of what this story tells you. One thing may be that I am a very poor decision maker, and that is true. And it may demonstrate the struggles I have experienced in trying to "live in and enjoy the moment" rather than worrying about life's what-ifs. But also, to this day, money and I have a rather acrimonious relationship. Since the time I began earning enough money to be comfortable, I haven't liked to walk away from something I *want* but really don't *need*, though I do manage to do it at least *some* of the time!

QUEEN OF THRIFT

By Cathy Peterson

"Because we don't have enough money" was a constant response in our home when we asked for things we wanted as kids. I never thought we were poor, because we owned a furniture business downtown and had a charming home with nice furniture. Dad was a hard worker and was always finding creative ways to make more money. Mom was a stay-at-home mom, as were most of the moms back then. Mom's job was to be frugal with the family money.

My shy grandma was what I called thrifty, a true penny-pincher. She reused everything, including plastic bread bags to keep her knitting projects in. She kept tinfoil and reused yarn, creating a true variety of colors in her inspired sweaters and vests she would gift us. She even took her ruined nylons and wove them into braided rugs. In her quiet way, she taught me how to be thrifty, too. Her special toys for us were old, pretty buttons and polished rocks she kept in a small painted bucket. Cheap maybe, but the most fun toys ever!

The changing point in my life, though, was when I was able to tag along with my dad up to Minneapolis one time to pick up a load of furniture. This was during the time I was a bashful, scrawny student in junior high. While we were up there, he took me to a used clothing store. I was in heaven. I found a greenish-teal 1940s lounging outfit made from exquisite, thick satin, and it was only $9.00 (I'd brought with me $10.00 I had earned). My dad let me buy it, and I felt so rich as the slippery fabric clothed my body. I dreamed I was a wealthy movie star lazily stretching out on a chaise lounge. I became hooked on used clothing due to that splendid feeling. Oh, that treasured outfit was way too big, but that didn't matter.

After getting through college and having gotten married, Charlie (my husband) and I didn't have much extra dough to spend, so I truly became thrifty. I sewed our daughters' clothing and especially loved designing and creating their little dresses. It seemed we lived on hot dogs, mac and cheese, pancakes, soup, barbeque, and Hamburger Helper, with which I could stretch a pound of hamburger.

After eight years of marriage, I became a single parent, and living sparingly became a way of life, especially since my ex-husband didn't think he needed to pay his meager child support. I was Old Mother Hubbard who went to the cupboard, and when I went there, the cupboards could be bare. Sometimes, I wasn't sure if I would have the money for a necessary gallon of milk. My daughters wore used clothing, as did I, from garage sales and thrift stores. I was becoming quite competent at stretching the almighty dollar, and I was still sewing all their dresses in addition to sewing matching dresses for their Cabbage Patch dolls. I never felt poor, though. Rather, I felt rich, because I had a college education, had good friends, was gifted with creativity, and would persevere. Living frugally was now a way of life that suited me. I've never clipped coupons, though, like so many other frugal cheapskates!

As the years went by, my enthrallment with living as cheaply as I could gave me the feeling of being challenged by the world. I was capable, and nothing would take away the realm of my responsibility and vigilance with caring for and providing for my children. It became a part of me and was in my blood and soul, so to speak. I had accepted this ongoing challenge to be prudent. At times, I was Scrooge collecting and counting my pennies, but it's paid off.

After another eight years, I remarried, but my lifestyle would not change. I delved even more into being thrifty. I had married Mr. Spendy, who had been raised with affluence, but I have never taken on being lavish or being a big spender. During this time, I was also going through many medical surgeries on my injured neck. The medical bills piled up, and monthly payments were difficult even though I had a good job. There was no such thing as saving money, especially not with raising teenagers!

During those years, as my children grew, they got involved in the school's theater productions. Their being characters in the plays gave me the unique opportunity to also be involved by sewing costumes. What fun that was! My pièce de résistance, though, was when my son was a senior and the fall musical was *Joseph and the Amazing Technicolor Dreamcoat*. I volunteered to be the head seamstress. Looking high and low in every thrift store within one hundred miles, I gathered sheets, blankets, tablecloths, curtains, shower curtains, bedspreads, and used fabric. I created and sewed all the costumes for Joseph, his eleven brothers, his father, and the other males in the production (eighteen in all, so about forty costumes), and then I altered the girls' costumes, too. I scrounged everywhere for what could be transformed into authentic-looking biblical attire. It was the highlight of my thrifty costume-making career.

Later, for ten years, I was also in charge of the Lenten drama skits at church, for six weeks each winter and spring. Recruitment became my middle name as I cajoled many congregational members into being the actors. I sewed all the biblical costumes needed to create the Old and New Testament look for the characters. Yes, each year all the costumes were sewn from thrifted items.

I'm proud to be frugal, economical, prudent, somewhat stingy, and a recycling, unwasteful penny-pincher who loves reusing anything and stretching money. I call myself the queen of thrift. My friends say I'm too frugal, but I'm not buying it! A sign in one of my favorite store says, "Friends don't let friends thrift alone." I love it! I've learned life can always be lived with less money, and being thrifty is always justifiable. Even Thomas Edison said, "The scope of thrift is limitless." Watch out, Goodwill! Here I come!

SPIRITUALITY AND VALUES

By Mary Lou Lenz

I went to Merriam Webster and found a meaning of spirituality that I liked. "It can be said that religion comes from the outside, spirituality focuses on the within."

Then I searched my funeral folder again and found this poem that defines some of what spirituality means to me.

To Laugh Often and Much
By Ralph Waldo Emerson

To laugh often and much;
to win the respect of intelligent people
and the affection of children;
to earn the appreciation of honest critics
and endure the betrayal of false friends;
to appreciate beauty;
to find the best in others;
to leave the world a bit better
whether by a healthy child, a garden patch,
or a redeemed social condition;
to know even one life has breathed easier because you lived here.
This is to have succeeded.

"To laugh often and much"
To see the humor in a situation is important to me and means I have not taken myself too seriously. I accept I could be wrong and that there

could be another side to a story. Wit and wisdom are two characteristics I cherish in friends.

"To win the respect of intelligent people"
We found our best friends on a field trip to the Minneapolis Museum of Art. They were sitting behind us on the bus and the wife kept introducing topics to talk to us about. Later on in the relationship, I asked her why she had pursued us, and she said, "Oh, we were new in St. Cloud, and I saw *The Progressive* in your husbands back pocket. I said to my husband, 'They could be friends.'" That was the start of our twenty-year friendship.

"To win the affection of children"
Our family values education. My husband and I were both teachers—he in higher education, while I taught preschool and adults later in life. After college, we took a group of Bishops Chorister's for a music and language camp. Before I taught family education, I taught religion in my home to high school students in an experimental "released time" program, and my husband and I taught many "Pre-Cana" classes to people contemplating marriage. Upon retirement, my volunteer work included starting a lending library at the Holdingford Community Center, teaching ESL, and being on the boards of Whitney Senior Center and the Chamber Music Society of Saint Cloud—still teaching from my experience.

"To appreciate beauty"
For me, spirituality includes a sense of wonder and an appreciation of things that can fill you up, the ability to feel, and the openness to see beauty in all its manifestations. I include here the appreciation of good art, good music, good nature, good writing, and beautiful objects. One time, a friend of mine said she could not live if she was not surrounded by beauty. At the time, I thought it was a pretty pretentious thing to say, but as I age, I think about how many times the spiritual has given me its gifts. I also love to be surrounded by people who appreciate the same things I do; it's another kind of being lifted.

"To find the best in others"

To me, to be spiritual, is to believe in the humanness of others—the "essence" of others, their innate goodness—as well as acceptance of their foibles. I believe another person has it in them to find their way out of a mess they may have caused. I believe their intentions are good until proven otherwise. I believe one should be open to loving, living, and acceptance. We should have the ability to seek forgiveness from one another when we haven't been our best.

"To leave the world a bit better whether by a redeemed social condition or..."

During our marriage, we had a banner in our house that said, "Planting a tree shows faith in the future." One way we showed our belief in the spirituality in nature was by this activity. We demonstrated our belief that leaving "the world a bit better" was important by planting forty thousand trees over our lifetime.

We also tried to demonstrate a social conscience to our children by actively participating in our community, for example, by starting, with others, the Tri County Human Relations Council, which was the forerunner for later such organizations in St. Cloud.

"Whether by a healthy child, a garden patch"

It is in hiking and being outside that our family always became rejuvenated. It was a time to solve problems mentally and to experience nature's beauty. The young children could run and play freely, and there was never a need for discipline or pettiness. We developed walking trails on our land, which one of our daughters further developed and maintains even today.

I have written about our two large gardens—we produced most of our own food during our small farm phase. Even though the four girls complained about their job of weeding one very long row of vegetables too often, two of them have done it for their own families as they become closer to self-sufficiency.

This poem does say it all for me. It closes with, "To know even one life has breathed easier because you have lived here. This is to have succeeded." Those words have sustained us and have kept us breathing easier for an entire lifetime.

CLINGING

By Mardi Knudson

breeze brushes against
brown brittle leaves
nudging

they nod, know what is to come
yet refuse to let go
cling onto life-giving branches

remember past warmth
buds of promise
simmer in summer sun

so too I reach for your hand
firmly grasp arthritic fingers
touched warm with heart-felt meaning

know letting go
signals a move toward our winter
snow and cold arrive

blanketing memories and life

A WINTER DATE

By James Ellickson

Our whirlwind romance continued. But let me digress with another story. It seemed to us college students that our forefathers were always conspiring against us.

Our college was designed to make dating especially difficult for students at the time.

First, there was the weather. The college was built on a hill west of town where the winter wind, after blowing unheeded for hundreds of miles, crashed into the hill with great frozen anger.

Then, the men's dorms were clustered in the northeast quadrant of the campus, while the women's dorms were clustered in the southwestern quadrant, with various common buildings like the library, the chapel, and the student union in between. And of course, student cars were forbidden at that time.

On an especially windy Saturday evening in January, we had arranged for a date. I put on my stocking cap, scarf, gloves, winter jacket, and my heaviest boots, and then I headed out for the trek to Ellen's dorm across campus. As previously arranged, we had an old blanket for warmth and provisions for a winter picnic.

About halfway across campus, we stopped at Old Main, the college's oldest building. We entered the empty building and closed the front door tight. We climbed the wooden stairs to the third floor and settled in to eat our picnic dinner, serenaded by the whistling winter wind outside.

About halfway through the meal, we heard the front door open and then slam shut. Two heavy winter boots clump-clumped across the wooden floor below and started to climb the stairs to the second floor. We sat in silence. They continued to climb to the third floor. I had to do something, so I called out, "We are on the third floor having a picnic."

The boots came up the stairs, and it was Bud, a well-known maintenance man, getting ready to close up Old Main for the night. We students called the maintenance men (as they were always men), the "Green Army." They were in a parallel universe from us, keeping the place operating, but largely unseen.

After looking us over, Bud told us, "Shut the door tight when you leave."

"Okay," we replied.

And then we heard the clump-clump of the boots retrace their steps down the stairway and finally out the door.

Thanks for all you do, Bud.

A Path Reaffirmed

By Steven M. Hoover, PhD

First published in *Onward!: True Life Stories of Challenges, Choices & Change*, Birren Collection, 2021

There are crossroads in life that offer trajectories and potentialities—new directions, possibilities, and promises. And then there are intersecting paths, coming at a time of personal and professional crisis which reaffirm life's purpose. My life and Richard's intersected briefly and intensely beginning in the fall of 1979. Entering my third year of teaching and my first year at Suncoast Middle School, I was in the midst of the challenges and disillusionment that face many new teachers—too many students, little support, and very limited income create the educational trifecta that leads 50 percent of new teachers to leave the profession in the first three years. We had left Indiana on a whim to escape a backwater town and a dead-end teaching job. Unfortunately, the lure of sun and sand did little to brighten or change the underlying issues of work that seemed less than a career.

I first met Richard and his parents at school orientation the week before classes began. Parents and students moved from room to room listening to an overview of the curriculum, viewing their classrooms, and meeting their new teachers. As Richard was in my homeroom and first-period class, he and his parents came to my room first that evening and arrived early—a habit I would soon understand was a survival strategy but initially irritated me, as I was caught up in preparations for the 120 students and their parents whom I would meet that evening.

Nevertheless, if one is fortunate, and present for it, there are crystallizing moments when our lives intersect with someone's hopes and dreams and give us the opportunity to grow. That moment came for me in the eyes of Richard's parents as they handed me a brochure on sickle-cell anemia and asked that I look it over and call them if I had any questions. Then, they thanked me and quietly took seats near the back of the room by the door, where Richard would spend his time in my classroom all year. So often, teachers become inured to the parents who inject themselves into our lives, advocating aggressively for their child and, in consequence, alienating the teacher and other parents. This was clearly not the case for Richard's parents. It was a simple request, for me to merely read a pre-printed flyer, one I could have ignored and immersed myself in the chaos that was my life.

Richard was one of the smallest students in my eighth-grade physical science class in a newly integrated middle school in North Fort Myers, Florida. He was one of a number of African American children who daily rode one of seven buses from the Dunbar area, one of the poorest and crime-ridden sections of town, to the redneck center of central Florida. Bus ramp and hallway fights were a regular occurrence, and a diminutive, chronically ill student was a potential target. On days when Richard could attend school, he made it his habit to come immediately to my first-period classroom to avoid the threats of hallways and lockers—sometimes carrying all his books in an overloaded backpack. The stress of physical violence, long, noisy bus rides, and carrying a forty-pound load constantly threatened, and often succeeded, in triggering episodes of his sickle-cell anemia.

I learned a little about sickle-cell anemia from that flyer, and a little more from the school nurse, who found some material that described the disease. However, my real education came not from books, pamphlets, or healthcare professionals, but from Richard, his parents, and his brothers and sisters. I learned about his dream to become a doctor and find a cure for his disease, both for himself and for other children who were afflicted. I learned that he desperately wanted to graduate from high school and that he knew he was falling behind due to his inability to manage the long bus ride and the full day in school. I learned that he was afraid he wouldn't even graduate eighth grade and get to attend high school. I learned first-hand what a sickle-cell crisis looked like and, through Richard, what it felt like. I learned what it is like to try to navigate a system that marginalizes a condition for which there is little hope and for which there is an implicit bias. I also learned that sometimes a teacher's job is not just about the content of the classroom, but about the relationships we have with our students' hopes and dreams and "the content of their character."

I learned about Richard's hopes and dreams at his hospital bedside and at his home as we worked on schoolwork, because he was too tired to navigate a day in school. I saw how his family supported his hopes and dreams even though they understood the reality of his illness. I laughed as Richard told me jokes that he had heard on the bus and that I was never to share with his mother. He asked me about college, and if it was hard, and if I thought he would be smart enough to get there and graduate. Sometimes, when he was sicker than usual, I would collect his homework from the other teachers on the team and send it on the bus, and then we would talk briefly on the phone at night, although his mother would generally intervene as he tired. Then I would offer her suggestions on how to help him with his math or science homework, and she would chuckle and hand the phone to her husband.

Richard did make it to high school. His parents and family, along with my teacher colleagues, made sure that he mastered what was needed to graduate middle school. However, the demands of the high school curriculum, his progressive condition, and an inability of the educational system to adapt to his needs meant that his eighth-grade graduation would be his last.

I have stayed in the profession for over forty-five years, continuing even now, in retirement, to teach seniors health-promotion and Guided Autobiography. Richard's was only the first of so many memorable roads crossed, but it came at a time of professional crisis and shored up the path that I have never left. I have been deeply in Richard's debt for these many years and so very grateful that I chose the path on which we met and never diverged from it.

SIT DOWN, YOU'RE ROCKING THE BOAT

By Tamara McClintock

When I was young, my mother told me a story about one of her relatives. It seems her father's uncle, Hakan Berggren, inherited the family farm following the death of his father. It was the custom in Sweden to deed the property to the eldest male heir. Unfortunately, Hakan was a gambler and had to sell the farm to pay off his gambling debts. This story made quite an impression on me, and I vowed I would never gamble.

My mother and father were never interested in gambling. They both worked hard for their money and wanted to spend it on important things like theater tickets (who *wouldn't* want to watch Alan Alda in a Broadway show, am I right?) and their children's college educations.

My sister and her second husband went to Las Vegas multiple times over the years. They spent their time exploring Red Rock Canyon, Zion National Park, and other nature spots, as well as going to shows. But the whole time they were there, they stayed clear of gambling. My sister hadn't been particularly shaken by mother's cautionary tale about Hakan Berggren but, having been an A student in math classes, she was savvy enough to know the odds aren't good in that kind of venue. Her math skills reaped monetary benefits when we were in elementary school. At Christmastime, she figured out a system for buying presents for Mom and Dad: we'd split the cost in half, even though she was getting a bigger allowance. (I didn't figure out why I was broke in January while she still had money until I learned about fractions in school.)

Years later, when I was living in Iowa, I was directing a production of *Guys and Dolls,* a musical about the attempt by the Save-a-Soul Mission group to reform all evildoers, including a group of gamblers. Life sometimes imitates art, and as the rehearsals progressed, I began finding parallels between the play and my surroundings.

In the county in which I resided, there was a controversial bond issue. Residents of three towns were eligible to vote. If the bond passed, a company would be granted permission to build a casino in the town of Riverside. For anyone who finds bits of trivia interesting, in 1985, Gene Roddenberry, creator of *Star Trek*, granted the Riverside city council's request to call itself "the *future* birthplace of James T. Kirk, Captain of the starship *Enterprise*." Once a year, this tiny berg was making a modest sum of money with their *Star Trek* festivals. However, they knew the really devoted Trekkies were going to the big-city conventions, where they could see the Kirk and Spock actors rather than some random actor who played an extra that got killed in the first five minutes of episode 25 by a gooey blob called the Horta. Hence, the town eagerly saw the casino as a more profitable "enterprise."

Seven miles from Riverside was Kalona, a picturesque small town, filled with Amish and Mennonite folks. There were also some very conservative churches in the area. It goes without saying that these groups were vehemently opposed to having a casino only seven miles away. Like Sarah Brown and her zealous Save-a-Soul Mission group in *Guys and Dolls*, these folks were vocal about the evils of gambling and saw the casino as a threat that would lead to moral degradation and corruption.

Close by was the neighboring town of Wellman. There wasn't a lot of excitement in Wellman, and the majority of the residents were all for having a casino in the area. Ignoring the dire warnings of the Kalona naysayers, they were perfectly willing to risk the possibility of sliding down hell's gaping maw.

Editorials about the casino appeared in the local newspapers every day, signs were posted on bulletin boards of local grocery stores, and there were reports about how hot the town hall meetings were getting.

My focus during this time was on rehearsing my show, and when opening night came, the cast was ready and eager to perform. The climax of *Guys and Dolls* comes in the big ensemble number, "Sit Down, You're Rockin' the Boat." The gamblers attend a church service at the mission, where they repent and vow to follow the path of righteousness. My actors really rocked this number, and night after night, the audience burst into cheers and thunderous applause.

Then, the following week, the overwhelming majority of them went out and voted yes to building the casino.

LIFE AND TIME

By Rachel Johnson

I listen to the Beatles on a sound bar connected to my iPhone. I am a rock and roll granny. I am sixty-six going on twenty. The mirror on the wall and the mirror of my soul at odds with each other. I remember my Grandma Nora telling me she didn't feel as old as her birthdays on the calendar. Now I know what she meant. Life and Time make strange bedfellows.

VIEWING MACHU PICCHU

By Roseanna Gaye Ross

These ancient Incan ruins speak.
     Are you listening?
Their voices carried across the valley
     On whisps of clouds
          Like fingers stroking the highest peaks
             disappearing . . .
               returning . . .
Revealing
     Stone terraces, an abandoned citadel
          a city of granite and limestone forged by Incan hands
             surrounded by mountains and protected by peasants
Telling
     Of Incan emperors and nobles?
          sacred ceremonies?
             a respite for travelers?
               a viewpoint for stars?
                    A sanctuary for the Chosen?
Mysteries
     Not fully known
          as thousands come in pilgrimage
             to explore
               to experience
                    to listen for

Stories
      lost in the whispers of "Old Peak" to "New Peak,"
           echoing across the tropical mountain forest,
                carried on the ripples of the Urubamba River below.

*Machu Picchu, in Indigenous Quechua, literally translates to "Old Mountain Peak," and Huayna Picchu literally translates to "New Mountain Peak."

Photo by Roseanna Gaye Ross

I Aspire to Travel?

By Jean Eulberg-Steffenson

There really was no choice. I had to jump down over five feet into the water or stay there the rest of my life. Our tiny guide reached out to hold my hand. I felt quite secure holding his hand that was the size of a ten-year-old boy's attached to his one-hundred-pound body. I screamed and jumped. Obviously, we made it. We paddled on the tubes until, suddenly, the river was without current. We had to hustle to get to the end. At that point, we had to hike over a mile with our tubes to our "cab." We (the Gringos) were seated on boards on the tail of an old, rusty pickup truck! They drove fast, and we bounced along the incredibly bumpy roads. The woman next to me was at the end of the row on the tailgate. Her face looked like she had just seen a horror film! A cop car was right behind us. I imagine it was his job to run over any gringos who fell off and remove them from the road. So much for our "relaxing tube down the river day" in Costa Rica. It had sounded *so* pleasant.

Previously, in Golfito, we had taken a hike that took over six hours. The hills were steep; the weather was excessively hot and humid. There were absolutely no points of interest or great views to see or wild animals. It was just more rain forest. We hiked by tree after tree. Everything looked the same. My body became drenched with sweat. Even my eyes stung from sweat. I could barely put one foot in front of the other to make it up the mountainous terrain. My daughter and the guide stood on both sides of me and pulled me up the hills. Later, my daughter heard the guide tell another he thought I wouldn't survive. My husband had booked this miserable tour through a recommendation of the owner of the restaurant where we rented out the back. So, we thought a pleasant time tubing a river had sounded fantastic. After arriving in Osa, we booked the trip. Oh, little did we know!

While we sat on the deck of a cabin in Osa, we watched monkeys swing through trees not far away. We decided to have a peaceful, calm day kayaking. Our strong daughter, who is a very experienced kayaker, was in one kayak, and my husband and I were in another kayak close by. Suddenly, the largest alligator we had ever seen moved very close to us! I imagined us watching our daughter's long, coal-black hair falling around her beautiful face as the alligator opened its jaws for her! Luckily, we somehow figured out how to avoid it and exited the water as soon as possible. Well, that was certainly relaxing!

We also booked a snorkeling trip. There were no docks, so we had to jump onto the boat. That was typical of our trip from Golfito to Osa! Going to Osa, on a large boat, we had to jump into the water and walk to shore when we arrived. In between, we had to catch a raft across a river. It had been an adventure just getting there. The snorkeling trip *was* pleasant. The views were gorgeous, the food was good, and we saw dolphins and colorful fish. However, after snorkeling, I had to have two people pull me into the boat by grabbing both of my arms! It was a jump up and grab on procedure for everyone.

Then we left for San Jose. After putting us on bunks in the back of a restaurant, my husband said I should choose where we stayed in San Jose. I picked out a place recommended by Tripadvisor. Our twenty-five-year-old daughter had flown home by then. We found our hotel. We passed many businesses and homes in San Jose with bars over the windows. Now that is not really a safe feeling! The hotel was close to a couple restaurants. We booked an all-day tour for the next day. In my room, I went back to read what they said recently about this hotel. I realized it was a center for "ladies of the evening" to visit! Oh boy! The room looked clean enough. I used the bathroom off the lobby and heard two men discussing their "adventures" with women. Their wives were "nothing" to them.

In the morning, my husband and I had breakfast and then took our coffee to a sitting room area. We watched with amusement as a lean, pretty, young woman with poofy hair and thick makeup climbed the staircase. She wore a short, tight dress and spiked heels. After about fifteen minutes, she climbed back down the steps with a man in his fifties behind her who looked a bit sheepish. She left the hotel. He put his head through the doorway of the sitting room we were in. He looked at us with shock as we sipped our coffee! His expression reflected his thoughts. We imagined him thinking, *Wow! This guy really isn't getting his money's worth!*

After a couple days in San Jose, we flew out to Pococi. It was lovely, and we did a night tour and saw many creatures of the night, including a tiny green frog whose venom is strong enough to kill humans. We stayed in a small resort, so it was somewhat normal for accommodations!

Many talk about their love of Costa Rica. It is true that beauty surrounds you, such as the flowers that are amazingly beautiful. When we stayed in the rooms behind the restaurant in Golfito, we had a delightful night kayaking trip where we viewed the luminescence. The luminous planktonic organisms caused a wave of tiny golden sparkles in the water, like tiny stars that fell from our paddles. We stopped and got out of our canoes. We walked into the ocean and viewed the light show as we moved our arms and legs in the water. It was magical. We went back in our kayaks. We crossed back to our restaurant hotel in the quiet darkness surrounding us, with the stars overhead and the tiny stars in the water with each movement of our paddle. It was indeed breathtaking!

So, I continue to travel to experience sights I thought only existed only in fairy tales, along with a few frightening, challenging adventures that make me aware I am still alive! We have since experienced earthquakes in Puerto Rico; a trip to Australia, where we needed to return home immediately due to the pandemic as our airline had shut down; bears following me in Canada; and buffalo following me in Yellowstone.

"Life is not measured by number of breaths you take, but by the moments that take our breath away!"

—Maya Angelou

IF YOU COULD CHOOSE ANY TALENT, WHAT WOULD IT BE?

By Patsy Magelssen

I am very happy with the talents God has gifted me, but, being human, we always yearn for something beyond what we have and often question God, as if He hadn't done a good enough job in our gifting.

I so appreciate the wonderful way he made my body whole. I'm not missing any arms or legs. My eyes are in the holes they are supposed to be in. Countless miracles were done in creating muscles, bones, a brain to think, and skin to cover the whole miracle. From the love between two humans and the planting of that egg of creation came the most miraculous, screaming, little kid!

I know deep within my being I could have any talent I chose, but I would have to work for it to be created. An artist doesn't just put pen or brush down on a paper and, presto, art appears. A musician doesn't just sit down at piano and beautiful music flows from his fingers. It is the same with any human achievement. Sure, some are more gifted in certain areas, but you have to sharpen and work at perfecting those skills. The problem is that most people do not want to take the time. I am one of them.

I will choose the talent I wish, such as singing. I want to sing like a bird, with beautiful melodies reaching up into the heavens. The angels will remark, "Where is that beautiful melody coming from?" God will even look over His shoulder and say, "Patsy, is that *you*?"

I will have a big grin on my face and say, "Yup, I finally took the time to learn how to read music." I was too busy enjoying all the multitudes of other gifts you gave me. I love to talk, laugh, run, and dance around. Keeping house, raising three wonderful children, and vacationing around the world took a lot of time. I love to sew and create gifts for children to send the love of Jesus.

And I do sing! Not great—in fact, off-key. Probably much too loud. But I don't even care. If someone at church does not like it, they can move to a different pew. I sing walking down the road, in the woods, in the shower, and driving a car. God knows making a joyful noise is praise to Him, and that's all that really matters.

No, I think I will choose counting. I have never been good at counting.

ONLINE DATE

By Brad Busse

I met someone online recently. Nancy was her name. We chatted a couple of nights a week for almost a month, and I really liked her. She was funny. And smart. And, most importantly, she laughed at my jokes.

We finally decided to meet up, but then a strange twist of fate happened. I suddenly got an invitation in the mail to a fancy cocktail party. Seems the local arts council was having a fundraiser and auctioning off pieces of art to the highest bidder. So, I swallowed hard and asked if she would accompany me.

Now remember, we had never met in person. So, I was as nervous about what she might think of *me* as I was about what I might think of *her*.

To my surprise, she accepted and asked what the dress code was. I told her no tux for me, as I was just wearing a suit and tie, and she said, "Oh great! What do you think about a little black dress?"

"Great!" I said, gesturing to me waist and neck. "As long as it isn't too tight around my waist and maybe has a Peter Pan collar?"

The night finally came, but when I arrived at the hotel, there was no sign of her. People were milling around, but no Nancy. Along with tables full of wares—pottery, clothing, crafty things, and the like—there was a large, life-sized sculpture covered with a black tarp sitting in the middle of the room. *Probably one of the pieces of art they are going to auction off,* I thought.

Suddenly, the sculpture moved. It spun slowly toward me, and I realized it was Nancy. Her little black dress looked more like a giant black muumuu. For a split second, the image of the turd emoji flashed before my eyes.

She sashayed toward me, smiling. I have to admit, the first thing I noticed was her smile, and it was more amazing than I remembered from her pictures. And those eyes! A knot suddenly formed in my gut. I hoped my face didn't give away my—for lack of a better phrase—shock and awe. I forced a smile and said, "You must be Nancy!"

"Yep," she replied. "Not what you were expecting, right?" Her eyes bore into me like laser beams.

"N-no," I stumbled. "I have to admit, I didn't know what to expect." *Good no answer, guy!* I thought. *Good no answer!*

"Don't like big girls?" she asked. "A few extra pounds turn you off?"

"No," I lied. But then again, not really. A woman didn't need to be Twiggy for me to find her attractive. I glanced down at my feet, amazed I could still see my shiny black Rockports past the stomach hanging over my belt. "Preaching to the choir, hon!" I laughed. "I have nothing to brag about myself!" I insisted, patting my spare tire. "In fact, I've decided to embrace my Buddha-like figure. I'm thinking about becoming a rapper!"

"Yeah?"

"My rap name will be Lil' Belly Pooch. What do you think?"

She threw her head back and laughed, and her laughter sounded like tinkling bells. Then, she grabbed my hand. Her face now had the definite look of relief etched on it. "Hold this," she said, placing a corner of her muumuu in my hand. "Now hold on tight!"

She began to spin around, slowly at first, then faster as the covering unwound and unwound, slowly revealing an average-sized woman with a mound of black cloth at her feet. She wore a simple blue dress that matched her blue eyes. She looked amazing. I used my hand to manually close my gaping mouth. Wow! I thought. She smiled at my reaction.

"So, what's with the tarp?" I asked.

"I wanted to see what kind of guy you really were," she said. "Not some vain jerk who can't get past someone's looks."

"Did I pass?" I asked expectantly.

"Almost." She grinned from ear to ear. "Your face at first was a bit . . ." she trailed off.

"Apprehensive?" I said hopefully.

"Okay, we'll stick with that," she giggled. Then, with a very serious look on her face, she said, "Let's go pig out at the buffet!" She glanced at my dumbfounded face and burst into laughter.

"We'll start at the salad bar!"

LONGING TO BE: A JOURNEY INTO MATURE MASCULINITY

By Steven M. Hoover, PhD

First published in *Homecoming: Personal Stories on the Search for Belonging,* Birren Collection, 2022

I was born into it. A time before it was openly questioned. A time before we even knew it existed. A time before social forces questioned, then requested, then demanded we see it, accept it, and, ultimately, own it. A time in which masculinity was created within the "box" that restrained and defined who we were, and, most importantly, who we were not. Like the proverbial fish that isn't aware of the water, the "box" just was. It was a time during which, for many of us, the journey was defined, the route laid out, and the outcome predestined. In order to belong, we simply needed to learn the rules, understand the dimensions, constrain our emotions, and follow the leaders.

For me, as for many young men, the journey toward masculinity began with my father. As my first model of what it meant to be a man, my father typified the traditionally masculine male of his generation. A man was a successful breadwinner, the protector of hearth and home, physically strong, fearless, emotionally stoic, sexually successful, and lord of his domain. As a young man I learned the rules and roles through examples and the consequences for behaviors that ventured outside the "box": men don't cry; we suffer our injuries, physically and emotionally, in silence; we are self-sufficient, we don't ask for, nor do we need, help. We solve problems, we don't talk about them. Actions, not words were our currency. We didn't need to say how we felt (we actually didn't even know how we felt). Our behaviors spoke for us. Why say "I love you," when we showed it daily? Feelings were for girls, boys didn't need them—they existed outside of the box—stuff them down, shut them off, act them out, but don't express them.

The rules for masculinity were strictly enforced, by our role models and by other boys: "Be a man, man up, men don't cry, men don't back down" were the messages men lived and died by. The rules of masculinity were also enforced by the girls and women in our lives, although they did so reluctantly and with a sense of our loss—weighing the costs and benefits of raising emotionally constrained men against the consequences of not preparing boys to live in the world of men. For most of my early life I belonged to what I felt was the masculinity I wanted even though I knew there were portions of myself that were out-of-bounds, suppressed, and relegated to quiescence. It was relatively easy to play the role, don the mask of masculinity, and banter with the boys. We all knew the correct words and acceptable attitudes toward various groups and girls. Even if we really knew that each of us probably didn't truly believe what we said, the risks of not belonging were too great. We lived fully within the confines of the pseudo-rituals of manhood designed to milepost the events in life that signify the transitions, if not spiritually, then physically and socially. Bereft of mature men to truly initiate us, we celebrated our milestones: driving license, high school graduation, draft card (we outwardly postured about our serving in the Vietnam War, while desperately hoping, and marching, for its end before we had to actually make the choice—Canada was enticingly close), loss of virginity, drinking age, college, marriage, job, and children. All the socially prescribed rites of passage that marked manhood. However, unlike my father's generation and those before him, there were cracks in the edifice, and, as it is said, "That which we resist, will persist." Belonging began, for me, through the mentorship of the men in my life, to being a socially acceptable man, but not yet a man-in-full. For that, one needs to return, to reengage those aspects of the self that were pushed outside the box. Those portions of our complete self, our anima, which we relegate to the darkness within found ways to emerge, and forces, external and internal, were moving toward a personal, professional, and marital crisis. For my ego to mature, I needed to be open to a different type of mentorship.

I was not alone in experiencing the changing forces that impacted men of my generation and, eventually, my father's. I was witness to the changing dynamic within my parents' marriage that should have been a call to awakening. As roles and economics began to shift with my mother's emerging independence and my father's tightening grip on the world he understood, the crack in their relationship blew open when she responded to his latest "my house, my rules" dictum with her "I no longer *need* you" retort. Then, in what I have come to deeply appreciate as a message of love and, more importantly, understanding, she followed up with, "But I still *want* you." A seemingly simple distinction we have all made with our children; needs versus wants redefined their relationship, placing it in a new configuration—one based on mutuality not dependency. She was my first model of the emerging feminine, the *anima* I had suppressed, the archetype who serves as a guide for men to reengage with those aspects of our complete selves that have been ignored in the service of the socially prescribed myth.

The second model of the secure, independent feminine who wanted, but didn't need, entered my life when I was still fully engaged in the process of living the masculine ideal. As I would press up against my wife's subtle (and sometimes not so subtle) teachings of what a mature masculine was, I discovered the limitations of my boy psychology. As I became more open to deeply listening to the alternative voices for change, like my father, I was forced to reconsider, then reject, and, ultimately, reengage a way of being that had once existed in me, in all men. I see this fully now in my six-year-old grandson and have hopes for him, as his parents want him to live the full emotional life that his grandfather and great-grandfather had lost, and then finally found.

MY JOB CHOICES

By Lolly Loomis

I grew up in what in those days was considered a traditional family. My mom was a homemaker, and my dad worked at a rubber plant and "brought home the bacon." As a result, the girls in my family were expected to do the housework, make the meals, and watch the younger siblings. The boys were expected to mow the lawn, take care of the car, and keep up the outside of the house.

As I grew up with these values, my decisions about my work life went something like this: Girls, in my way of thinking, could be nurses, secretaries, or teachers. I didn't want to be a nurse, because I didn't want to give shots, clean up nasty messes, or watch someone die. I thought about being a teacher, but I figured I'd never be able to go to college. No one in my family had ever gone to college. I was the oldest of seven children, and though we had a comfortable life, there was no extra money to send me to college. My decision was made. I would be a secretary. I figured I would work a few years, then get married, have a family, and become a homemaker like my mother. While in high school, I learned to type and take shorthand. I also worked in the office as a student helper in my senior year.

Well, things started changing in life and in my mind. A new movement started called Women's Lib. Although I didn't buy into everything they said, I did like what they said about women having the same opportunities as men. More women were choosing to continue working even after marriage and family.

What I discovered about myself was this: I didn't want to be a secretary all my life. I wanted to go to college and be a teacher. I discovered my good grades in high school could go a long way in helping me get to college. I got scholarships and grants. I also received money from social security because of my dad's death. I received this money once I graduated from high school as long as I was in school. I lived with a family friend that first year and paid minimal rent. So I went to college, and four years later, I was a schoolteacher licensed in both elementary education and special education.

I did get married the summer before my senior year, and a few years later, I had a family. I took time off from teaching to raise my children while they were still young. I always appreciated that I could do this, because another reality was apparent. Many of my female friends had no choice. They had to work in order to pay the bills.

This, I was sure would be my life's work. I really enjoyed teaching, and I was good at it. Then my life went through another change. Through all of this, I had always been intrigued with the law. At the age of sixty, I went back to school for my paralegal certification. I found the work fascinating, and I did very well, graduating with a 4.0 grade point average. I had two teachers, and my advisor asked me if I ever thought about being an attorney. I must admit, I had. However, the thought of going to law school and starting a new career at the age of sixty-four did not seem right. My answer to my advisor was, "Maybe if I was forty."

So, there you have it. I was a lifelong teacher and an attorney wannabe. If I'd been born twenty years later, maybe I would have been an attorney. My choices were influenced by my own upbringing and the roles men and women played in society at that time. Don't get me wrong, I loved teaching. I feel I contributed to my charges' lives in a positive way. However, I still wonder sometimes, *What if?*

Choosing Life

By Jean Eulberg- Steffenson

I love this picture of us together! You looked so fashionable wearing your silver-colored suit that flatters your lean body. My hair was straight and somewhat stylish. On my face was a grin like a jack-o'-lantern's. Your lean face surrounded by your light-gray hair contained a more sophisticated, gentle smile that brought out the bright blue of your eyes.

Your wise, humorous ways were always delightful. You had three very energetic, adorable sons. I followed suit, having three sons after you had yours. You always desired a daughter. I listened to your comments, which encouraged us to adopt a daughter from China over twenty years ago.

I carefully listened to your advice on how to raise children, how to be capable of constant change, how to cook, etc. Patience and the ability to respond without anger with a carefully formulated, thoughtful response were your strengths. With your wild, humorous, restless husband, you moved frequently, and vacations were shorter than expected. A weekend in Duluth with us was actually just one night. You handled it all.

Thank God we didn't foresee the future. We planned a great visit eight years ago. The guys and my daughter were going hiking. We were going to have a great time playing tourist and visiting your new home in Helena, Montana. But the world had changed drastically for you since our last visit years before. You were not awake yet, so I left with the men for breakfast our first day there. They quickly left for their hiking trip. You woke up and couldn't remember how to make coffee. You said that it was a new pot. They are all different, so I didn't think much about it.

We started discussing sights to see in Helena. You said you weren't sure. Then you stated we could visit the grocery store, but you weren't sure how to get there. Your refrigerator was filled with yogurt. We went to the grocery store, and you bought only yogurt. Outside your condo was a street vendor, and you bought frozen yogurt. We went to a nearby restaurant. You had been a gourmet cook, but you said there was really nothing on the menu, although there were many delicious items. You ordered yogurt.

I was able to figure out a few sights for us to visit. You pulled on a very warm wool sweater and long pants. You were surprised you were hot in the eighty-degree weather. You had difficulty making conversation, which had always run smoothly between us.

One day, your son invited us to watch his son play ball, but you thought it was too hot. Your lovely little granddaughter visited, but your joy for a little girl had disappeared.

Ah! Your son and his wife took us and his family into the mountains. You had mentioned a mountain visit, but I was not comfortable traveling with you. I was very grateful your son drove us in the mountains for a day.

"Did you notice anything different about Jeannie?" my husband asked on their return from their hiking trip. After two days of hiking, Larry had informed him about Jeannie's dementia. We'd had no clue before. I was a bit angry at Larry for putting me in that position, but I realized how desperately he must have needed a vacation.

Within a couple months, you became very mad at Larry. You hit him and asked him to stay away. Your kind, patient personality no longer existed. You ended up living with your son and his family. You called me once to complain about how naughty your granddaughter was. After a year, you entered the nursing home. After four years, your life ended with breast cancer.

I recalled years ago your desire to go to a Fleetwood Mac concert. So, we coerced our husbands into going. As Stevie Nicks sang, she danced around the stage in a flowing, black chiffon dress. "Oh, I just want a dress like that to swirl around in," you said. I could tell you saw an image of yourself whipping a lovely dress around as you danced. What a delightful thought.

Once diagnosed, her three sons came to visit. Dan lives in Helena, Jon lives in Alaska, and Eli in Minnesota. Each of them has an adventurous personality and could be a challenge when they were young. The three men stood by her side. She had not responded and had been catatonic for many months. Jon, the shortest, with bright red hair and freckles, was by tall Eli with his own bright red hair. They had inherited their hair from their mom. They stood next to medium-sized Dan, with his coal-black hair. As they gazed down at this woman they loved so dearly, who had dedicated her life to them, her eyes fluttered open. "My boys!" she said, and then quickly shut her eyes, not to open them again. She died within a month.

At one point, she had been an RN for Mayo Clinic doing research. It is so difficult to see someone lose their memory. Life sometimes throws us a curveball we can never hit. When she died, I felt I had gone through her death already. However, I realized I hadn't, since memories kept popping up and flooding my thoughts.

As we age, we find we have more friends with serious medical issues. While facing an aggressive breast cancer two years ago, I had an extremely close friend with heart failure. Due to the pandemic, we rarely saw each other. We talked on the phone, and she said, "We will get through this together! We will have a wonderful time once we are healthy and can get together!" She had always looked thirty years younger than she was and was one of the kindest women I knew. She rarely mentioned her health. So, it was easy to forget how sick she was. The day I started my four months of chemo, she died. It made me sad every time I thought about us getting together again. Although, truthfully, I would prefer *not* to meet her again for a very long time! I am not excited to enter the afterworld yet.

How do you handle it when you are diagnosed with a fatal disease? My friend's husband (a retired physician) survived three years of knowing his cancer was fatal, yet he remained extremely cheerful and loved discussing other events. He enjoyed playing his guitar and concentrated on that instead of his health. I asked him how he managed to stay so positive. He replied that you don't have a choice about your illness, but you have a choice about how you handle it. If you decide your health is your only focus, people will be tired of listening, and you will always be filled with constant sadness. If you focus on other issues and find some happiness in activities, you will be living your life and not letting cancer control it.

I have been told my cancer has been "melted" and my odds of a recurrence are slim. However, my Facebook sisters fighting the same disease often find out differently. So, I am cautiously optimistic. Therefore, I have decided to live my life, try to do whatever I really want to do, and visit people who are important to me. The pandemic affected that. However, I still try to spend time doing what I enjoy or can appreciate. Above all, I rarely skip dessert!

The Day That Changed My Life

By Jean Eulberg-Steffenson

An immense jolt smashed against my body. I hurtled through the air as my world turned black and an explosion of pain engulfed me. I plunged to the frozen pavement. Screams surrounded me. In my mind, I could see my picture and the word "death." I was only fifteen, and I doubted I would survive.

My eyes slowly opened. I gazed up at the faces of my neighbors. There was Vicky, who I walked to school with. Her plump, usually cheerful face reflected shock and horror. Next to her was Mrs. Scanlon, the little, trim, proper principal's wife. She bent down next to me. Her short, gray hair was blowing back from the raw wind. Her narrow eyes held intense fear as she gently spoke to me. "You were hit by a car after I stopped to give you a ride. Are you okay?" A strange man in his twenties appeared numb at the sight of me. He was in shock after hitting me with his car on his way to work at the local bank.

Waves of excruciating pain raced through my leg. "No," I replied. "My leg! Oh, my leg!"

She grimaced as she looked at it. "Don't worry. We will get help soon."

Suddenly, my two older sisters appeared. They were home from college. Their long, dark hair billowed around their beautiful faces as they ran toward me with tears streaming down their faces. Before crouching down, they hastily wiped their tears and changed their facial expressions to appear calm. Mrs. Scanlon informed them she had stopped on this twenty-degrees-below-zero day to give us a ride. Vicky and I had both started racing across the road. I was in the lead and was hit.

Blankets were placed on top of me as we waited for the ambulance. Underneath me was frozen ground. I heard rumors about an ambulance.

They could not find the driver. This was 1967, and cell phones were non-existent. The main ambulance driver was also the mortician of our small town. The non survivors continued onto the funeral home instead of the hospital. It was a profitable business. It was so profitable that the entire family was in *Europe*! In 1967, in our small town, that was as unheard of as a trip to Mars! However, there was an ambulance driver/mortician replacement for him *somewhere*!

They searched for over an hour as I lay on the frozen pavement. Finally, the principal decided he would drive me to the hospital in Rochester himself. Minutes after his arrival, the ambulance pulled up. The substitute had been having his morning coffee in the café down the street. He loaded me up efficiently, with my sisters hovering on both sides of me. We started off down curvy Highway 52 to Rochester. On each curve, I rocked and the bone in my leg pushed toward my skin. I moaned in anguish, and I prayed the bone would not go through my skin. My sister Pat looked at me critically. Appearances were important to her, and she always resembled a model. Her lips pursed. "Didn't I tell you that you should wash your hair last night? Now, you are going off to Rochester without washing your hair!" Hearing these words from anyone else, I would have assumed I was hallucinating. However, I knew she was concerned, particularly if anyone recognized me as *her* sister!

My oldest sister, Susan, grinned as she held my hand. I closed my eyes. I heard them whispering. "I can't believe that she will ever walk again," said Pat as she viewed my swollen blue leg. We continued our forty-mile drive.

"Who is that man?" the ER doctor hollered as he examined me. I looked over and saw my dad's handsome face surrounded by black, curly hair and a large pair of glasses perched on his wide nose as he peered around the curtain.

"That's my dad!" I replied. The doctor changed his tone and let my dad in. After an extremely long and thorough exam, they determined my leg was broken. The bone had been crushed into many pieces. I was told many times I was lucky to be alive.

My lovely, concerned mother arrived from work accompanied by my two frightened younger sisters. They were bawling. One was a seventh grader, and the other in third grade. They told me through gasps that friends had said I was run over by a steamroller and was dead! Their sweet, young faces were filled with tears of relief.

I was hauled away and shared a room with a young RN for two weeks. Surgery involved placing a plate and pins in my leg. I had frequent flashbacks during that time. I felt the entire experience again, including every ounce of pain. It was like a 3D rerun you wanted to avoid. I cannot imagine what veterans go through.

Due to a huge lack of technology, the main source of communication for me was mail. I received many letters we laughed over. One started out, "Dear Jean, are you dead?" Others asked how I survived being run over by a steamroller!

I think everyone in my small class of fifty wrote to me. I had only lived in Preston for a little over two years, and I was still considered "the new girl." I was basically shy and lacked confidence. So, the letters definitely impacted my recovery and self-esteem. They were kind and made me feel appreciated.

I was forced to talk to adults in the hospital, including the young RN who was my roommate. Afterward, I kept in contact with her through letters. She urged me to enter a medical field, but after my experience, I *hated* hospitals!

A few decades later, due to this injury, my ankle was wrecked. There was not any cartilage left. I had pain and could barely walk for a few years. Luckily, a neighbor who had a daughter who was a sports medicine physician referred me to an orthopedic surgeon who specialized in ankle replacements. That surgery has allowed me to walk many miles and to appreciate every step I can take!

A Fork in the Road

By Martha Johnson

On the eve of October 26, 1993, I was nine months pregnant and was en-route to St. Cloud for a 2:00 p.m. to 7:00 p.m. shift. It was chilly outside, and the leaves had already fallen from the trees. All of a sudden, two large deer ran out of the ditch and onto the road. Instinctively, I swerved into the oncoming traffic, and before I could make it back to my lane, I had a head-on collision with a Chevrolet Blazer. The windshield shattered into what seemed to be a million pieces. The car's floorboard got pushed toward me and caused major injuries to my legs and ankles. The next thing I knew, my car was in the ditch, and the airbag had deployed. I could not breathe, as the force of it had knocked the wind out of me. My thought was that if I got out of the car, the cool outside air would stimulate me to breathe. I was in pain all over, especially my ankles and my abdomen, and my feet were at a right angle to my legs.

I managed to open the car door and maneuvered myself into the ditch. Someone had already called 911, and, in a short period of time, I heard the emergency vehicle's sirens. They were screaming down the county road and could not get to me fast enough. The medics put me in a neck stabilizer and on a backboard. The two-mile ride to the emergency room seemed to take forever! I hurt more every time we hit a bump in the road. The time I spent in the ER was extremely chaotic, with supplies and people racing all over the place.

As I was being stabilized, I could hear my baby's heart rate on the fetal monitor that had been put on me. Being an obstetrical nurse, I knew there was not much time left before my baby would die. I was taken to the operating room after saying goodbye to my family, who were at the hospital by then. I underwent an emergency C-section and had my ankles and a broken leg repaired. My baby was limp and blue and not breathing. They did CPR and assisted her with breathing. She was then rushed to the neonatal intensive care unit. It was a very long surgery! My husband was able to see me in the recovery room, and at that time told me Gretchen was beautiful. We did not know the sex before then but had picked that name in the event the baby was a girl. She was absolutely beautiful and weighed eight pounds. After two days on a respirator, she was doing better and was taken off it.

Over the next ten days, I developed terrible abdominal pain and was taken back into surgery. I was in shock by that time. It turned out I had three intestinal perforations the doctor had not found because he'd made the wrong type of incision. After that surgery, I developed septicemia, which is an infection within the bloodstream, and subsequently developed adult respiratory distress syndrome. I spent eight days on a respirator, which required me to be in the intensive care unit. I had casts on both legs. Consequently, I could not bear weight on my legs at all. This was going to be a long rehabilitation.

Gretchen's health improved, and after two and a half weeks, she was discharged. I, on the other hand, was in the hospital for a total of five weeks. I came home to a hospital bed in my living room and medical supplies all over. My mom lived with us for three months to help with my and Gretchen's care. Gary, my husband, worked full-time and helped care for Megan (seven years old) and Bentson (four years old) when he was at home. Our church organized a number of people to bring meals to our home, which was of great help. Home health nurses came every day for quite some time. In addition, I was in physical therapy two to three times per week for about a year. Two more surgeries were in my future.

It was a long rehabilitation and a major stressor on my family. We did get through it. Needless to say, my life changed drastically when I swerved to miss hitting the deer. In total, I was out of the workforce for twelve years, and I knew I would never be able to do many jobs in nursing because of my orthopedic injuries. I also have other residual physical issues that have resulted in numerous health issues and periods of illness. I had abruptly become a stay-at-home mom with almost no preparation.

As I reflect back on this life experience, there are positive things that have occurred because of my accident, too. I was fortunate to have stayed at home with the children while they were young. The whole ordeal removed me from nursing for an extended period of time. I had been burned-out anyway and was so relieved I would get a reprieve. My nursing career consisted of positions that were outside the hospital and was, as I perceived it, the winding down of my career as I knew it.

Lastly, I met Diane, who became a dear friend to me. She has truly been a gift. Gretchen is now twenty-nine years old, is married, and has three children, Natalie, Mia, and Keegan. The best part is that she has no apparent problems from everything her little body went through. Someone had been watching out for us and gotten us through a horrific period of time in our lives. That makes me incredibly happy!

2020 VISION

By J Vincent Hansen

A reflection on sustained affluence

That we
had managed
to hold up
so high
for so long
so many things
testifies less
to inordinate strength
than it does
to the fact
that the things
we chose to elevate
were hollow.

COURAGE

By Patsy Magelssen

Strength to persevere: Do we have it or not? Will that strength be available to us at the time we are tested, or will fear overpower us? We will not know until that moment of testing. Will we fight or flee? It depends on how strongly you feel about the challenge and if it is worth your own personal integrity to make a stand for or against.

Personally, I have had many times when I've been put to the test and lived to tell about it . . . It still sends shivers up the back of my neck recalling one of those times in particular.

I had signed up for a trip to Venezuela with nine others to bring eyeglasses to a clinic for those in need, deep in the mountains. We brought with us thousands of pairs of used and donated eyeglasses collected by the men's Lion Club. We set up our clinic with the doctors in a part of an old school building. The doctors prescribed the optical readings and sent them over to us to fill the prescription in the main building.

I love taking things along on trips for the little children, so I had several suitcases of puppets, duffle bags, and McDonald's toys to give them while they waited in line for glasses. As this was a free clinic, people waited in long lines all day for the chance to be seen. During our lunch break, a young boy of about twelve years old pestered us for several days about taking us to see a beautiful waterfall in the jungle a short ways away. He assured us we would be back in a half hour.

After much urging, two of the doctors, myself, and another man said okay and started out with the boy and three other little guys into the jungle. I noticed the leader of this group wore brand-new, leather, high-top boots, and I commented on them . . . strange, in a country where the average salary of a working man was two dollars a day. It took a machete to cut us a trail through the vines and bushes, and after over an hour, there was still no waterfall in sight. The temperature read over 110 degrees, and Dr. John offered me one hundred dollars for my bottle of water, which I shared. I had never been so hot!

Just then, the most beautiful, eight-inch-long, bright blue butterfly came drifting by and landed close to the path. It was, for sure, a *National Geographic* beauty. I took out my camera and started focusing in on it. (Now this was 1993, with a camera of those years). As I stood bending over the bushes, I felt a hard object hit my head and looked up to see a *pistol* held to my head—by the boy! He was speaking Spanish, so I didn't know what he said, but I imagined it was the money in my fanny pack he wanted. No way was I going to give him my passport, identification, tickets, and money. I played dumb and raised my hands. The only words I knew were *gracias* and *momento*. That didn't work. He pulled the trigger. The gun clicked, and the bullet carriage went around a space. I was sure I would be dead in a minute and prayed like crazy. I opened my eyes, and I was still standing right there in the jungle . . . the rest of the group walking about forty feet ahead of me! The gun pushed harder into my scalp, and the same demanding Spanish words were angrily said. Again, I repeated my two words, pleading for some time. The four men in my group contin- ued walking farther away, and the gun trigger was pulled again . . . *click*. You cannot imagine the fear that raged through my body. But the third demand was the last straw. I said, "*Momento, gracias*" and then *screamed* as loud as I could, "Dr. John, I NEED HELP!" He turned around and ran as fast as he could, shouting Spanish at the kid and demanding the gun.

He grabbed his arm and wrestled the gun from him. Dr. John twirled the cartridge around, shook his head in disgust, and said, "Patsy, you scared me half to death! This gun doesn't even have bullets in it!" He yelled at the kid in Spanish and gave him back the gun. And you know what? That kid put it back in the duffle bag I had given him back at the school. See if I ever give that kid anything again!

The whole trip was a challenge of one's stamina. We woke up in the morning with roosters on our open windowsills crowing and had to shake the tarantulas out of our shoes before putting them on. There were big iguanas and howler monkeys living in the trees. Huge, bright-colored birds squawked when we went under the branches. I did inquire if there were piranhas in the rivers, but no one knew for sure.

Each day, the bus drove us down the mountain with tires so bald, they had no tread. Our village did have a huge waterfall, which we walked behind on a little rock ledge. One day, we took a trip and forged rivers, pulling on a big jute rope to cross. We flew in a small, five-passenger plane, one which the pilot had to wire the plane tail on before takeoff to secure it. Up and over mountains we flew, even over Angel Falls, one of the world's highest waterfalls. The final day, we toured a huge cave in which there were large Guacharo bats hanging on the ceiling, and I came home sicker than a dog.

It took over six months on four different antibiotics to finally get back my health. It was quite a trip. I didn't get the picture of that majestic blue butterfly, but it will forever be emblazoned on my mind.

EIGHTY-NINTH TRIP

By Jerry Wellik

we met 50 years ago
Floyd W. Ayers, firstly
my teacher and advisor

always there for me
nudging me to be
the best version of me

excited and quick to
notice any little bit
of improvement

next we became
colleagues working
and learning together

Best of all friends
celebrating his 89th trip
around the sun

Floyd Ayers and Jerry Wellik

Saging Not Aging

By Mary Lou Lenz

I began to live and die on November 3, 1939.

I celebrated my eighty-first birthday with a tea for my eight best friends, plus my granddaughter and great-granddaughter. As I looked around the table, almost all the women were younger than me—two older friends had moved to live with family in the Twin Cities (St. Paul and Minneapolis). Our topics of conversation were typical—whether to move or stay in present housing, current aches and pains, surgeries, travels, latest books read, family stories, etc. Many in the group were friends acquired as a member of the American Association of University Women (AAUW). This group has answered most of my needs as an aging woman—friendships, intellectual stimulation, role models for my future (although I wouldn't mind if some of them would slow down a little), and emotional support. And through its lobbying efforts on the national level, AAUW allows my one small voice to take on the power of a very powerful voice on important women's issues.

The other groups that have offered both social and intellectual stimulation are the humanities group and more recently the guided autobiography group at Whitney Senior Center, as well as our family, friends, and neighbors, who keep us aware and among the saging.

In no particular order, I will list what I have learned about growing older thus far:

- We all demonstrate our age uniquely. As in every other stage, each of us grows at our own pace.
- We are forever learners and still have curiosity, hope, and questions, but often only a few answers.

- It's okay for us to sit in the chair and read, write, and sleep—as long as we move some throughout the day and communicate in some way to others. *The Week* is a great magazine for those who seek the many sides of an issue in a shorter format. Energy will show up one of these days.
- When we fail at something, we must forgive ourselves.
- It takes us longer to do *everything*, even dressing. But we should continue to do it.
- We might expect some aches or pains every day, but don't dwell on them because they usually go away in a short time—if they don't, then seek help. MyChart is great in the meantime.
- On a related note: I have accepted over-the-counter drugs into my life.
- I am allergic to noise and conversely love peace. One of our daughter's caregivers called ours "the quiet house."
- Don't treat me as one of the herd, I am still very much a person.
- Ask me if I want help but have the sense to not overdo it.
- I rarely feel dismissed by people, but I have learned to see it as their loss if they don't seek to include me and my opinions.
- Keep yourself surrounded by children. Our neighborhood currently has children from ages one to eighteen, and they are some of the wisest among us.
- My appetite for good food and wine is still alive. I'll enjoy until I can't.
- Many of us know what loss is. Be available to those who are new to it.
- Being alone doesn't need to mean being lonely. The inner strength we've developed will go far in sustaining us when needed.
- Having a mate is a gift. Never take it for granted and always take it into consideration when addressing those who don't.
- Retain empathy and don't get bogged down in your own problems.
- I want to be told the truth by those who know it.

When visiting one of my heroines, who taught Latin to a small group of admirers when she was ninety, we were walking down the hallway, and she asked me to slow down. Thinking she couldn't keep up, as I was in my agile seventies at the time, I apologized. She said, "Oh, no—I wanted to look at this United States map. I am memorizing the States—I was always weak in geography."

I keep her in mind when I remember this short saying by Mary Lamberton Becker: "We grow neither better nor worse as we get older, but more like ourselves." I suppose that is why our ninety-year-old friend fell off the roof he was repairing and why I sometimes say inappropriate things.

I recently began rereading *Aging with Grace: What the Nun Study Teaches Us About Living Longer, Healthier, and More Meaningful Lives* by David Snowdon and want to end with a quote from it. "Aging is a time of promise, and renewal, of watching with a knowing eye, of accepting the lessons life has taught, and, if possible, passing them on. Beyond survival, we hope to remember, to have someone to whom to express our thoughts, to remain independent, to be spared the suffering caused by chronic illness, to live with people we love and who love us, and to continue a future filled with hope."

Lines In Response to Rumi

By Roseanna Gaye Ross

Be a lamp or a lifeboat or a ladder
—Rumi

If I could see through the thick mist
    that clouds my thoughts
        And sets me adrift . . .

If I could float effortlessly
    Upon the ups and downs of the frightening waves
        Like a nymph in the sea . . .

If I could reach beyond the gray abyss
    Above the rushing waters below
        To the top of the cliff . . .

Then I would not need
    Your lamp
        Nor your lifeboat
            Not your ladder.

Perfect Pandemic Age

By Barb Flynn McColgan

I never thought I'd see the day
That I'd just sit back and say
"67 is the perfect age for me"

But, then COVID-19 came,
And it quickly changed my frame
Of reference -of what my life should be

When told that we must quarantine
It didn't make my income lean
I'm glad that I am a retiree

Social security in my bank
Pension check—both these I thank
For giving me COVID security

No kids at home to educate
No job on ZOOM to orchestrate
Online classes were an opportunity

No illnesses that preexist
Helped reduce my COVID risk
(Though "COVID weight" is not the best for me)

When your age begins with number 6
And the time comes for vaccine picks

Your vax comes quicker than if you were 30

This age that once sounded old
I now see is pandemic gold
This year, it's been the perfect age to be.

About My Good Friend Carl

By James Ellickson

My friend Carl passed away last year.

We met in kindergarten, at Windom Elementary School in South Minneapolis. Our moms were both nurses, and somehow all the nurses in our neighborhood knew each other. I remember Carl had shiny new shoes with very deep treads, which must have impressed a five-year-old. I remember those shoes.

The city built a new elementary school, Sister Kenny, to remember all the kids that had gotten polio. Little did I know at the time, but Ellen's little brother, Mark, had polio about the same time. Anyway, living on the west side of Lyndale Avenue, I went to Kenny Elementary, and Carl stayed at Windom, as he lived east of Lyndale.

We met again at Ramsey Junior High School, growing up again on parallel paths. But then the city built a new Susan B. Anthony Junior High School, and off I went on a different path, while Carl stayed at Ramsey.

We met again at Washburn High School and again at St. Olaf College. We married our best girlfriends and went off to grad school. This was short-circuited when we each received our draft notices, and off we went into the Army.

This was where our paths widely diverged. Carl went to advanced infantry training, (101st Airborne Division) and then to the war in Vietnam. I worked in an Army data processing unit in a deep tunnel in the Panama Canal Zone. It was very safe duty!

Carl tripped on a land mine, but luckily it was slow to ignite. He took two steps before it went off, but he survived the blast.

Carl's wife flew with a lot of other young wives to Hawaii to see their husbands for some R&R. There was not a dry eye on the flight back to

CONUS for the ladies. The flight attendant announced they had just run out of water, so all drinks would have to be free.

Carl completed his tour of duty, then he burned his Army clothes and went back to civilian life. But the Army demanded more from Carl, this time as a reservist, so he had to buy all new replacement uniforms.

We both went back to our lives and our work. We each completed a career of civil service, Carl for Hennepin County, and I for the federal government. When the time was right, we retired. My wife, Ellen, got a job teaching nursing in Central Minnesota. I followed her, and we bought a hobby farm in the country. I saw that Carl's wife had become a dean at St. Cloud State University, so I stopped by her office. The outer-office folks wanted to know who I was and did I have an appointment. But she happened to see me and called out "Jim?" and gave me a big hug. I have never felt so important.

The four of us started to meet for dinner, twice a year. They would drive out to the country, or we would drive into the Big City.

One such trip was different. Carl and Suellen drove out to see us, and they seemed subdued. Carl had been told he had the kind of cancer that was due to exposure to Agent Orange. That was the chemical agent used to defoliate the jungles of Vietnam. They didn't know what they were going to do . . .

I survived the war by getting a cushy job in Panama punching cards. My brother survived the war by being brave as he called in artillery rounds on the enemy. But Carl didn't survive the war, in the midst of his service. We miss him.

LOSING A FRIEND

By Ann Romanowsky

Losing a friend slowly, sadly, certainly
Like air slowly leaving a balloon,
or light slowly leaving the end of the day.

A buoyant beauty moving with grace
dancing on currents of wind,
the balloon softens, sinks, no longer soaring.

But grace and beauty remain,
slowed now and at eye level,
tethered to the earth.

We gather around,
appreciating solid ground
before she's airborne.

TEMPTRESS OF TIME

By Rachel Johnson

The Temptress of Time
With her glowing face of Perpetuity
Grows more lovely with age
She gives what we take
Then with hostess-like grace
She kindly takes our leave

Friends of Mine

By Martha Johnson

Throughout my life, I have met many different types of people. I am gregarious and have no trouble forming connections with others. Wherever I am, I smile and greet people. Often, I strike up a conversation. I even greeted a couple of men sitting outside a sports store once only to realize they were statues. So much for forming friendships with them.

During my junior high and high school years, I ran with the same kids, doing what young people do. After high school graduation, those friendships fizzled out. I have only encountered them again at reunions. I have no regrets about not keeping in touch, as our journeys in life have taken us in different directions.

In the fall of 1976, I embarked on a new chapter in my life called "the college years." I lived in a dorm my freshman year at the University of Wisconsin–Madison. There were plenty of activities to attend, and, in a short period of time, a number of girls and guys from my same dorm started hanging out together. Slowly but surely, a strong bond developed. Our group experienced both highs and lows, and we were always supporting each other. The good times far outweighed the bad times. Most of us live in the Midwest, so we rendezvous from time to time. It is always fun to reconnect, reminisce, and share what is new in our lives. I really value my college friends and know we will always stick together.

Other people who I consider friends of mine include family members. My children—Megan (thirty-six), Bentson (thirty-three), and Gretchen (twenty-nine)—are definitely three of my best friends. I thoroughly enjoyed them as they were growing up and am having lots of fun now that they are young adults. Others friends in this group are my siblings. I wish I could say we are best friends, but sadly, that is not the case. I am close to my three younger siblings, Philip, Seth, and Sarah, but feel more like friends with my older siblings, Amy and Grant.

I also have two people in my life who are extremely special—true gifts. Kathryn is a fun, vivacious, loving person I met through a mutual friend about twenty-five years ago. Diane is an angel who was actually sent as a church visitor when I was hospitalized after a serious car accident. That was back in 1993, so it has been twenty-nine years since we formed a bond. These two amazing, beautiful women have laughed and cried with me. They have stood by me and supported me though many life experiences. I can bare my soul to these friends without being judged. They are priceless.

Last but not least, I have a dear male friend, who is the sweetest guy I have ever met! He has short black hair and goes by Chico. He is fifteen years old and lives with me. That special guy is my cat! The love I get from him is amazing. I am grateful I have had such a cool pal who rarely leaves my side. There is nothing like unconditional love.

Friends can be gained, but they can also be lost. Three people from my college group and two cats of mine, Ella and Nina, have already passed away. But the most painful losses I have endured were two of the best friends anyone can have—my mom and my dad. I was a mere eighteen years old when my dad died. We missed out on a lot! My mom lived to be ninety-two years old and was a bright light in my life. She was almost always happy and loved life! I miss all of these friends. However, I have great memories of them. I have been blessed!

The greatest gift of life is friendship, and I have received it.
— Hubert H. Humphrey

A good friend knows all your stories. A best friend helped you write them.
— Anonymous

Why Did It Take a Pandemic?

By Barb Flynn McColgan

When schools, stores, and businesses shut down at the beginning of the pandemic, we had been living in our house for thirty-one years. None of the neighbors around us on any side had lived here nearly that long. No one, that is, except Jeri, the widow who lives across the street. She's been in the neighborhood for forty-five or fifty years. She is currently in her seventies, and her husband died seven years ago.

Though we have talked at the ends of our driveways or in passing, it was only once quarantine started that my husband said, "It must get extremely lonely for Jeri. Should we stop over and check on her?" And so, we did. We wore our masks and, after knocking, we stood far back from her door. She came out wearing her mask and stood on her front stoop. We asked how she was doing and if she needed anything. We asked if her kids and their families were staying well, and she asked about our sons. And as simply as that, a new routine was established. Every day or two, usually after going for our walk, we stopped over and knocked on her window, then backed up double the required six feet. After she opened the door, we spent the next ten to thirty minutes chatting about COVID, politics, family, local events, about whatever was of interest to any of us.

When Easter arrived, I filled a plate with dinner and took it over to Jeri. I placed the Ziploc-enclosed meal on the step, knocked on the window, and backed up to await her arrival at the door. She was surprised and delighted at my delivery. Six months into the pandemic, when elective surgeries were allowed again, I had my knee replaced. After about a week, when I could go outside with my walker, the first walk I took was across the street to say hi to Jeri. We repeated holiday dinner deliveries on Thanksgiving, Christmas, and New Year's as well. In the cold of winter, our doorstep visits became briefer and less frequent, but we still stopped by to check on her and say hello. Now that we can all get out more, we don't visit Jeri as often, but we still stop over, knock on her window, and wait for her to come out and chat.

Jeri is a bright, informed, thoughtful, kind, delightful person. We have lived across the street from each other for thirty-one years. Why did we have to have a pandemic before our visits became routine? Why did it take a pandemic for us to get to know her better? The fact that my husband and I are both retired now certainly gave us more time, but we had already been retired a couple of years when the spring of 2020 rolled around, so retirement wasn't really the reason for this change. I believe once we were required to stay at home and isolate from others, we had more time to consider what kind of things were most important in our lives. Rather than letting activities and schedules and other people's ideas of what we *should* be doing just sweep us along, day after day and week after week, this isolation made us stop and think. It made us re-examine and recognize our true values and *choose* what we wanted to do with our time.

Many times during the last couple of years, my husband and I have talked about how lucky we are to have our health and to have each other, especially in a time of lockdown. We've thought about the many people in our lives we value and appreciate, and we've thought about the people we appreciate but take for granted. As a result, I wrote thank-you notes—to the gal who has cut my hair for years, to my pastor, to the mailman—letting them know I realized how much I appreciated them and I wanted to tell them so.

That is why we now *choose* to go over to say hello to our wonderful, longtime neighbor Jeri, rather than only visiting when we *happen* to run into each other by the mailboxes. I do not know a single individual who does not feel better when they know others value and care about them. This is how we let Jeri know she matters and we care about her. And when she opens her door wide, with that appreciative smile on her face, we feel cared about, too.

ANOTHER OBITUARY

By Roseanna Gaye Ross

Another obituary—
A colleague,
A friend.

My eyes burn
         with soft tears of loss.
My throat tightens
         strangling silent sobs.

I live with the recognition
of the fragility of days.

Like a dry, shriveled leaf,
         golden, brown-edged
         tossed along an upward path toward a darkening sky
         by a silent, icy breath.

This age.
The one that reminds me
daily
that there are fewer moments ahead
than behind.

When did I become
this age?

What happened to days
    When each new light
    Brought with it the warmth of
Life-breath,
    A meandering road approaching a far distant radiant horizon?

Silent sobs . . .
    falsely for others?
I ask myself . . .
    for whom do these tears fall?

Death's Miracles

By Lolly Loomis

I have experienced death quite a few times in my life. Some were close rel-atives—my father when I was seven, my mother in 2010, and two nephews who committed suicide at the ages of eleven and nineteen. There have also been several friends and neighbors along the way. Each of these deaths had a different effect on me. However, the death that had the most profound effect on me was the death of my husband, Gary, on October 8, 2016. Gary and I had been married for forty-six years, and we'd lived in the same house for the last forty-three of those years. We knew he was dying because his heart valves were no longer functioning due to a systemic infection. After a surgery to repair them on March 14 (my birthday), 2015, we got an extra year. Gary did well during most of that year, and we had a wonderful year together. By the following March, Gary's aortic valve "exploded." There was nothing else the doctors could do.

I now need to leave this story with a little aside. I thought long and hard about how to approach the topic of death. I knew I wanted to talk about Gary, but I didn't want to just rehash his death. I needed to give some basic information, but then I wanted to take a different angle on this story. There were two things that happened that, to me, are nothing short of miraculous. These two incidents had an even more profound effect on me because I believe life goes on after death. Death is merely a transition between this life and the next.

About a week before his death, Gary asked me to contact the kids and their spouses for a meeting with them, without the grandchildren, as he wanted to talk to them. I called my oldest son and told him of his father's request. I asked him to contact the other kids and set up a day and time to meet with his father. I told him it would be at our house. I also told him to make the meeting sooner rather than later.

They set up the meeting for the following afternoon at 3:30 p.m. The night before, on Friday, our youngest son came with his wife and family. On Saturday morning, after spending time with Grandpa, the children were taken to a friend's house in town. My daughter, who had to work that morning, dropped off her two children at our house for the morning. They had quality time with their cousins and their grandpa. After work, my daughter took her boys to a friend's house for the afternoon. My oldest son had told me his wife would not be able to make it to the meeting, because she had already set up a birthday party for their daughter at 5:00 that afternoon. At about 1:00 p.m., his wife drove up with all four kids. She stated that she thought it was important for her kids to see and have some time with their grandpa. After a few hours, she left with their kids.

The meeting was held for only the kids and their spouses. This was Gary saying goodbye. He had a message for each of them. As he could no longer talk loudly, he would whisper to me and I would convey the message to each person. Everyone was gone by 7:00 p.m., and Gary died two hours later. On that last day, Gary had a chance to spend quality time with each of his kids and their spouses, as well as all eight of his grandchildren. None of the time with grandchildren had been planned. It just happened that way. I believe that when it's time for you to die, you have a little control over the exact time. Gary's family was everything to him. The fact that God gave Gary this time with them on the last day of his life felt like a small miracle to me. He could say, "It is finished."

The second little miracle happened shortly after Gary's death. The mortuary people had put his body in a beautiful, quilted bag. We, the family, were gathering to say a prayer. The time was 12:45 a.m. Then a phone rang. I looked around. The phone ringing was Gary's phone. It was in the opposite corner of the room. I picked it up, and the caller ID said Gary Loomis. For a split second, I thought Gary was calling to say, "This is Gary. It's all a joke. I didn't really die." I pressed the answer button and said, "Hello? Hello?" No one was there. It was just an open line. All the kids and mortuary people were staring at me. I hung up the phone and told my kids, "That was your dad. He says to tell you he's fine." Now you need to know something else about that phone: it had no power! It had not been charged in weeks! Every time I tell this story, I still get goosebumps.

So, in painful times, when I am missing Gary, I think about the good times we had. I think about the children we raised together and the grandchildren we love to be with. I also think back to these two little miracles, and I smile.

A BLESSING FOR THOSE WHO GRIEVE

By Roseanna Gaye Ross

A blessing on the heart of those who wander the dark shadows of loss—
Their burden heavy in the face of that which is missing, was never there,
  or was tragically taken away.
Theirs is the silent longing, the daily wondering, the unexpected tears, the
  navigation of emotional turbulence.
Ours is to bear witness.

May the blessed angels guide you through the shadows,
Embrace you during the darkest nights,
Lessen your burden,
Wash away your confusion,
Be your constant companion
On your journey to your light.

Pandemic Shopping: Or Does Anyone Know of a Treatment Program?

By Barb Flynn McColgan

I can't completely blame quarantine. I mean, I did do *some* shopping online before we had to shelter-at-home. But when the only time I went anywhere was once a week to the grocery store . . . well, I *might* have gotten a bit carried away.

Instead of browsing the aisles of Target or Kohls, I browsed the websites of oh-so-many stores. I especially liked to explore the limitless options on Amazon. Once I had placed an order, I could watch and wait with bated breath for it to arrive. I signed up for text notices regarding delivery dates, as well as having my daily Informed Delivery email from the postal service tell me what was coming in the mail that day. It was like having a whole new sport to follow! Go Team Internet Orders!

Which item was supposed to arrive on which day? Will it come early or late? United States Postal Service, UPS, or FedEx? I could send packages to other people without going to the post office! I could look for the exactly right version of something and have it sent from anywhere in the world. Oh, the challenge of it all! I could experience the thrill of victory (orders successfully delivered) without the agony of defeat! Or so I thought.

Of course, then the bills started arriving, and the true cost of my new hobby became all too clear. Perhaps I'd better find a new sport to follow. Or better yet, another job!

I hope they have a post-pandemic treatment program for this addiction. I think I need it.

ON DEATH AND DYING

By Mary Lou Lenz

By the time I was sixteen, two of my favorite people had died, my four-year-old brother and my seventy-four-year-old grandpa. I witnessed both of their leavings, and I decided there was more I had to know.

At sixteen, there were things about my grandpa's death that mystified me: Why were people laughing and talking at the funeral when it was the saddest day? Why did the morticians seem to take over the day when my parents were perfectly capable? Question one could be answered by knowing the type of person my grandpa was: he loved laughing and making people happy, so he would have wanted it. The answer to question two: death sometimes renders you helpless and often not capable of making the smallest decision.

My mom was especially devastated by her young son's death. She cried at every meal we had for a long time. She eradicated any signs of my little brother—pictures, clothing, everything was gone. I was warned not to cry in front of my mom, because it would make her sadder, so I had no outlet for my grief. My mom mourned his loss until the time of her own death.

Because I disagreed with some of the ways death was handled in my family, I made it a mission to read, talk, and listen about the topic. Basically, I wanted to talk about it.

Through the years, I've had the opportunity to do just that. When I was a young preschool teacher, I researched and wrote an article for a professional magazine on dealing with death with preschoolers. This prepared me for many conversations with the parents of young children about how to treat the topic with those varied age groups. After retirement, I had the chance to be part of a group of role players for the SCSU nursing students, so they might have some idea of death and their reaction to it before facing the real thing. I was part of these two to three-hour sessions four times a year for about ten years. I also attended as many talks on the subject as I could.

After the funeral of a friend, which was really well done, I started collecting poetry, music, and ideas for my own funeral and that of my husband. It always seemed like such a gift when I would hear something so achingly beautiful that I had to keep it. Little did I know that we would use some of the contents of that folder prematurely, when our fifty-four-year-old daughter passed on August 9, 2019. I have also used the folder to send words to others who have faced a loved one's death. Recently, I sent my favorite poem, W. H. Auden's "Funeral Blues" (or "Stop All the Clocks") to a young pregnant woman and mother of one who lost her husband. The poem speaks to the absolute devastation one feels when a loss like this happens.

Stop all the clocks, cut off the telephone,
Prevent the dog from barking with a juicy bone,
Silence the pianos and with muffled drum
Bring out the coffin, let the mourners come.

Let aeroplanes circle moaning overhead
Scribbling on the sky the message "He is dead."
Put crepe bows round the white necks of the public doves,
Let the traffic policemen wear black cotton gloves.

He was my North, my South, my East and West,
My working week and my Sunday rest,
My noon, my midnight, my talk, my song;
I thought that love would last forever: I was wrong.

The stars are not wanted now; put out every one.
Pack up the moon and dismantle the sun,
Pour away the ocean and sweep up the wood;
For nothing now can ever come to any good.

I don't think Auden should have stopped there, because that painful, breathtaking kind of grief gets better for most people. And I do believe love lasts forever, even if one party is gone. Auden makes us think life cannot go on after a loved one's death, and that is too final for me—it eliminates hope. But I do like his use of natural elements, because it is in nature that I feel the most spiritual and thus closer to the one gone.

During the preparation for our daughter's funeral, I ridded myself of one myth; I believed funeral home involvement should be limited at the very most and the "salespeople" would very possibly pressure the bereaved into making expensive purchases while they were hurting. However, the funeral home we dealt with was more than happy to just do the cremation. They didn't push anything, such as having a gathering at the funeral home or buying their rather expensive containers. Years ago, I do remember a rather pompous director with clichéd rhetoric, but our helper was sensitive in every way.

So, I am pretty good at talking a good game, but I don't really know how I will accept my own death. I am already thinking about missing my family and friends.

About my own death—wouldn't we all want to leave peacefully, perhaps in our sleep? I hope people will say, "Why did she have to go so young? What will we do without her? She meant so much to me." For me, I hope I have lived a good life guided by the golden rule. I hope I have treated others as they would have me. I have tried to be a good mom to my children, a good wife to my husband, a good friend to my friends, a good volunteer who seeks out those who seem to need me the most. My mom was a longtime hospital volunteer, so she instilled that in me. I hope my children and their mates will miss me, remember me forever, and honor me by carrying out some of my values in their own lives, as they have already started to do.

As she lay dying, my mom, who was a good Catholic her whole life, admitted to me at one point that she wasn't sure she believed in life after death. That shook me, because she was so committed to the rules of the church. For years before and since, I have wondered the same about life after death, because acceptance of the principle required a belief in the unknown I no longer had. But I have always been inspired by the idea that *if* there is no life after death, we humans should live the best life possible. I hope I am.

ON DEATH, DYING,
& THE WASHING OF WINDOWS

By J Vincent Hansen

A found poem

Dear Vince,
The last time I was in Albany
Aunt Ursula gave me a clipping
of Mama's obituary.
I made some copies
and am enclosing one for you.

Earl doesn't change much.
He did take in the Host
When I brought him Communion yesterday.
He just sleeps
through Bingo and the Rosary now.

Carol, next door
helped me wash my windows today.
The weather has been so nice. I hope you are O.K.

Love,
Your Sister Rita

SHOPPING IN THE TIME OF A PANDEMIC

By Deb McAlister

Waiting in a long checkout line at Sam's Club, all of us wearing masks, missing the usual banter among others in line, more difficult with our mouths covered. A small voice behind me: "Hello, Teacher?" He looked vaguely familiar, but it was hard to tell with his mask. "Do you remember me from school?" Short man, Spanish accent. "I am Aldo, you help me with English grammar."

"Yes, of course," I replied, although not entirely sure.

"I know you by your eyes," he said. And although our mouths were covered, our eyes connected, his brown, mine blue, and they were smiling.

FATHER TIME AND ME

By Faye Schreder

When I glance into my full-length mirror, an unfamiliar woman peers back at me. I wonder who she is and how she got there. She certainly doesn't look like me! I wish I could evict her and replace her with the younger, slimmer resident who used to be there. I suspect Father Time may have had a hand in this duplicity.

For most of my life, I've had a fairly congenial relationship with Father Time. He kept his place in the background, appearing only at discreet intervals to mark milestones such as birthdays, weddings, and anniversaries. I liked him in that role. It wasn't until recently that he's become more meddlesome; some might call him adversarial.

In my younger days, the thought of growing older seldom crossed my mind. Oh sure, I saw its progression in the lives of my mother and her friends. In middle age, they began to add a pound or two here and there. Dark hair streaked with silver, and girlish figures became matronly in the colorful housedresses and flowery aprons. Still busy, but with their pace slowing, they laughingly teased each other about the old gray mare who "ain't what she used to be."

I seldom considered how their generation might be feeling about Father Time. Living well into their nineties, surely they must have had issues with him, too. As they aged, I still felt young. Oh, I may have had a gray hair or two, and those creases in my face were laugh lines, of course. Surely, I'd have plenty of time before I became his target.

As the years passed, Father Time intentionally dispelled such myths. I wouldn't have thought of him as being the sneaky sort, but what happened? When did it become my turn? I was just living my life, minding my own business, when he began to poke his nose into my affairs.

I discovered he has a sense of humor and likes to tease, but I find his jokes are mostly at my expense! First, he shrank all my clothes and doubled my waistline, then twisted my favorite shoes so they no longer fit. He also borrowed some inches from my height and replaced them in my width. He's been tampering with my face, too. It's never been the best one around, but I was used to it and didn't complain. Now, I definitely see that his agenda includes more than simply laugh lines.

Father Time's favorite direction seems to be south, and in many ways I concur. I like to go south for the winter, turn my face toward southern breezes, maybe even take a sip of Southern Comfort now and then. But I don't appreciate his audacity in rearranging my body in a southerly direction.

He has broadened my vocabulary with words like Aleve, face wax, trifocals, and Clairol. As I deal with each term, others are waiting in the wings. Actually, I'd like to bargain with him; I will try to accept whatever else he throws my way if he will leave my faith intact and my memory alone. But he refuses to offer any guarantee.

To be fair, I must admit Father Time has provided me with warm and joyous gifts only he can give: old friends, children, grandchildren, and great-grandchildren. Lately, he's also been giving me more of an appreciation for humility, accepting and forgiving my own faults as well as those of others. He has taught me I needn't fear him, that my steps may falter but I can still stay in the race. He reminds me to hang on tightly to each day, all the while giving myself away.

A wise old friend once said that when we age, our beauty steals inward. I hope that's true! If so, perhaps it's time for me to set aside my grievances, stop complaining, and consider a reconciliation between Father Time and me.

VOLUNTEERING: A CONDUIT TO HAPPINESS

By Lalita Subrahmanyan (an AmeriCorps RSVP volunteer)

An AmeriCorps RSVP (Retired Senior Volunteer Program) volunteer I interviewed once said to me, "This is the best 'job' I've *never* worked at," after which he went on to explain how he's never been happier volunteering, that is, providing services to others for which he does not get paid.

What wouldn't we all give to be happy? Leaders from various spiritual traditions remind us the greatest desire of all human beings is to be happy. Psychologists persuade us that happiness, a consequence of positive mental health, stems from a sense of fulfillment and belongingness, connections with others, high self-esteem, and the absence of anxiety. AmeriCorps Seniors RSVP volunteers and service recipients have reiterated on many occasions that these are the very benefits they derive from serving others.

RSVP surveys have shown consistently that volunteers feel a strong sense of connection. Volunteers feel a sense of purpose and are confident they make a difference. Furthermore, they assert they will recommend RSVP to anyone who wishes to volunteer. Such is the power of volunteerism: a sure conduit to well-being, augmenting social connectedness, self-fulfillment, and self-esteem, while eliminating anxiety, loneliness, and depression.

Volunteerism through directed programs can foster happiness in those who volunteer *and* those who are served. **The latest AmeriCorps Seniors RSVP Happiness in Action Initiative** is one such program. Funded by

AmeriCorps and the American Rescue Plan, this program is designed to create intergenerational partnerships between Central Minnesota volunteers and residents, working together to promote happiness and enhanced mental health to all ages. RSVP Happiness in Action ambassadors are trained and equipped with wellness tools from the Bounce Back Project, a health promotion effort powered by CentraCare. The ambassadors then use this training to organize guided service projects through which participants experience a spirit of kinship, satisfaction, success, and "Happiness in Action."

There are many examples that point to volunteering as a source of fulfillment. Meet a mother and daughter pair who contacted the RSVP office one windy Wednesday. The daughter was anxious about her mother's loneliness since her father's passing. "My mom needs to get out of the house and have things to do," she said. Soon after, the mother called. She was not sure about driving to the Whitney Senior Center, having relied for so long on her husband to take her. Yet, just a few hours later, upon visiting RSVP and meeting the staff, their fears were allayed, and the mother's loneliness transformed into happiness. All it took was a volunteer gig at Catholic Charities and the beginnings of a circle of connections with other women who had lost their partners. A first step forward had been taken.

Filing taxes can be difficult for any of us, and for the elderly, it can become a nightmare. The goal of the AARP Tax-Aide program is to mitigate those fears. Vicki, one of the volunteers, is happy when she sees all the people who come to get help "leave with a smile under their masks, relieved to have their tax-filing chore behind them."

Bev, an RSVP volunteer for many years, is an outstanding example of someone who has strived hard to alleviate food insecurity in her community. A list of achievements sufficient to make one's head spin shows Bev's indomitable spirit and untiring devotion in ensuring a caring service experience for clients at a food shelf where she was the former director. Bev, who volunteered for more than fifty years, until she retired recently, inspired others to join her and attracted numerous volunteers simply because, as she says, she never turned away anyone who offered to help and always found something suitable for them to do from the very beginning. When asked what she would tell potential recruits, this no-nonsense woman said, "I would tell them there's plenty to do. And it's better than sitting on your butt moaning and groaning about dumb things!"

Jim, an RSVP volunteer, exudes lightheartedness and caring when he talks about his volunteerism as fun and pleasurable. When asked in an interview what words of wisdom he would share with others about volunteering, Jim replied without hesitation, "I'd tell them volunteering is kind of fun, it's something to do, and you are helping somebody!" In other words, a perfect formula for happiness.

Biographies

Brad Busse
I was born in Omaha but grew up in Minneapolis, then Rochester, then Michigan, and finally Nashville, Tennessee. After college, I got a job in television. We moved back to Minnesota over twenty-five years ago, and I have been involved in and around theater ever since.

James Ellickson
Jim grew up in South Minneapolis and went to St. Olaf College, where he majored in mathematics. He met and married Ellen in 1967, and they moved to Maryland, where they pursued their careers and raised two children. In the year 2000, they returned to Minnesota. They currently live in Northfield, with an elderly cat.

J Vincent Hansen
I grew up on a farm east of Sauk Rapids. After high school and three years in the army, I spent seven years working as an agricultural volunteer with the Maryknoll Fathers in East Africa. I currently live with my wife in Sauk Rapids.

Steven M. Hoover, PhD
Steve works part-time as the Healthy Aging Coordinator for the Central Minnesota Council on Aging. A former member of the Board of Directors of the American Men's Study Association, he serves on the Board of Directors of Minnesota Men's Sheds Association. He leads courses in Guided Autobiography as well as Health Aging for Men. He lives in St. Cloud, Minnesota.

Martha Johnson

I grew up in Edina, Minnesota, and obtained a nursing degree at the University of Wisconsin. Throughout the next years, I married, had three children, and held a position in obstetrics/gynecology in Little Falls, Minnesota, then transferred to St. Cloud Family Birthing Center. After eleven years, my career ended due to a serious accident. A few unfulfilling jobs after rehabilitation compelled me to get a business degree from St. Cloud State. I was employed in office-related jobs until my retirement. I never envisioned traveling this path but also don't believe I would change any of it if given the chance!

Rachel Johnson

I was lucky to share my vocation and avocation in genealogy research. I realized after my work in family research how important leaving a legacy is. I am a wife, mother, and grandmother. My hobbies are writing, embroidery, and traveling.

Mardi Knudson

Mardi Knudson has been writing poetry for over forty years, originally typing annual birthday tributes to her sons on onion skin paper. She lives with one foot in the city of St. Cloud, Minnesota, and the other in the woods with her husband at their off-grid cabin near Ely, Minnesota.

Mary Lou Lenz

Mary Lou was born in 1939 in LaCrosse, Wisconsin and was educated in Wisconsin and Minnesota. She married an interesting man in 1960. During the middle of their marriage, they bought an old farm. Four daughters helped plant the fields in a wildlife planting. Mary Lou taught in preschool and family education, retiring in 2002. She is currently volunteering and living as a retiree in St. Cloud, Minnesota.

Lolly Loomis

Born in St. Cloud, I am the oldest of seven children. I got married in 1970, and I have three children and eight grandchildren. My husband passed in 2016. I currently live in independent senior apartments and spend my time in various activities, especially those related to singing. I spend as much time as possible with my family.

Patsy Magelssen

An eighty-two-year-old homemaker who loves life! Having grown up on a little dairy farm during the depression, she knows what it is like being poor. She uses her sewing skills to create thousands of gifts through Trash to Treasure, a nonprofit group since 1979, that makes gifts for children and nursing home residents from business cast-off fabrics. Passionate about creating little dolls for the Samaritan Purse/Operation Christmas Child shoebox program, she is called a "changemaker."

Deb McAlister

I am a teacher and a learner.
I am a daughter, a sister, a mother, and a grandmother.
I am a lover of family, humanity, and poetry.

Tamara McClintock

Tamara McClintock has spent her life doing the two things she loves most: teaching and directing or acting in theater productions. Tamara taught English, speech, and drama in various high schools in the tri-state area for several years. When back in Minnesota, she became involved in theater productions for GREAT Theatre in St. Cloud, Great River Arts in Little Falls, Great Northern in Cold Spring, and The Barn in Willmar. She also teaches an ESL class for adults at Quarryview.

Barbara Flynn McColgan

Barb Flynn McColgan in fifty words or less: lifelong Minnesotan married to an Irishman from Derry, two amazing sons and their wonderful partners, one adorable grandson, retired pediatric physical therapist with a master's in education, theater lover and amateur actor, traveler, wannabe writer, cross-country skier, card sender, reader, talker, always seems to be late, people lover.

Cathy Lee Peterson

Growing up in Southwest Minnesota, I began writing when I was young. For over twenty years, I worked as the community education coordinator/ director for two school districts and then as administrator for two non-profit organizations while raising three children. This past year, I began volunteering and writing stories after my husband and I moved to St. Cloud. I love sewing, flower arranging, and reading.

Jannine Provinzino

I am a retired secondary language arts teacher. I enjoy books and poems, good movies, plays, and travel. I love time shared with family and friends.

Ann Romanowsky

Ann Romanowsky moved to St. Cloud in 1978 when the Mississippi River exerted an undeniable pull on her husband. It still does. Her education as a nurse was enlarged and enriched by her two poetry teachers, Jerry Wellik and Frank Kazamek. They were inspired by the poet William Stafford, who wrote a poem every day.

Jim Romanowsky

Jim Romanowsky is a neurologist, fisherman, and amateur musician who joined the poetry group taught by Jerry Wellik a few years ago. He enjoys trying to put into words the scenes, sensations, and reactions to the events of daily life, sometimes with a photo of what inspired the poem.

Roseanna Gaye Ross

Roseanna Gaye Ross, PhD, is a professor emerita in the Communication Studies Department at St. Cloud State University, Minnesota. A member of Story Arts of Minnesota and the Minnesota Poetry Therapy Networkers, she recently joined the Whitney Poets group. Roseanna volunteers as a community mediator and conflict coach, providing communication and conflict-management training and consultation.

Faye Schreder

Faye Schreder grew up on a small farm in central Minnesota. The sixth child in a family of twelve, she, too, is the mother of a large family. She returned to school when most of her children were grown, graduating from St. Cloud State University at the age of fifty. She is a retired special education teacher living in St. Cloud, Minnesota.

Patricia Scott

I've been married for forty-eight years to George Scott. I always enjoyed writing at school and wrote short biographies about local businesswomen in 1979 for the *Wellspring*, a feminist newspaper in Colorado Springs. I retired in 2018 from my job as a psychologist in Brainerd, Minnesota, and took the Guided Autobiography class online in 2021. I also write annual Christmas letters, since my family and friends are scattered all over the country!

Jean Eulberg-Steffenson

I grew up in Iowa and Southern Minnesota. Married almost forty-five years, I am a mother of four adult children and now live in Onamia. After graduating from SCSU, I worked as a school speech/language clinician/ therapist. I worked in Hayfield, Minnesota, and then in Milaca Schools from 1976 to 2012. Luckily, I had ten years of part-time work to be with my children, my most important job. I write as a hobby, along with walking daily, reading, theater, and kayaking!

Lalita Subrahmanyan

Lalita Subrahmanyan is a professor emeritus in education at St. Cloud State University. She currently spends her time volunteering for various nonprofit organizations in St. Cloud and caring for her mother, who lives in Chennai, India. Lalita moved to the US in 1988 after having been born, raised, schooled, and later employed as an educator in India. She has fond memories of her life, her family, her childhood, and her experiences, exciting, poignant, and occasionally, nerve-wracking.

Jerry Wellik

Jerry Wellik is a professor emeritus of special education at St Cloud State University. His loves include poetry, storytelling, and practicing QiGong.

Elena Bookstrom White

Elena Bookstrom White taught dance for over twenty years in a variety of settings including community education, the College of St. Benedict, and the Perpich Center Professional Development Institute, where she also coauthored the "Dance Education Initiative Curriculum Guide." She holds a BA in American Literature from Middlebury College and an MA in English from St. Cloud State University. Elena enjoys skiing, dancing, reading, her sons, and the outdoors.

WHITNEY WRITERS AND POETS

First row from left to right: Martha Johnson, Elena White, Cathy Peterson, Rachel Johnson, Barb McColgan, Patsy Magelssen, Lalita Subrahmanyan

Back row from left to right: Debra McAlister, Tamara McClintock, James Romanowsky, Ann Romanowsky, Jerry Wellik, Patricia Scott, Mardi Knudson

Not pictured: Brad Busse, James Ellickson, J Vincent Hansen, Steven M. Hoover, Mary Lou Lenz, Lolly Loomis, Jannine Provinzino, Roseanna Ross, Faye Schreder, and Jean Steffenson

Made in the USA
Monee, IL
07 May 2023